THE GEN X AND MILLENNIAL GUIDE TO A THRIVING CAREER

AL SMITH III

iUniverse LLC
Bloomington

THE GEN X AND MILLENNIAL GUIDE TO A THRIVING CAREER

iUniverse books may be ordered through booksellers or by contacting:

iUniverse LLC
1663 Liberty Drive
Bloomington, IN 47403
www.iuniverse.com
1-800-Authors (1-800-288-4677)

ISBN: 978-1-4917-1151-4 (sc)
ISBN: 978-1-4917-1152-1 (e)

Library of Congress Control Number: 2013918800

Printed in the United States of America.

iUniverse rev. date: 03/21/2014

CONTENTS

INTRODUCTION

My first real job after college introduced me to the world of sales. I had no prior sales knowledge, but I was eager to learn and to climb the corporate ladder of success. Unfortunately, this new world was foreign to me. My employer did not provide a guide on how to be successful in the company, which was unsettling because I had just left three and a half years of college and the security blanket of a course syllabus and textbook. Did you have more questions than answers when you started your first job? Call me crazy, but I found it frightening that I had to figure out how to advance my career on my own.

These were unchartered waters for me, so I reached out to friends, family, and mentors for advice. The most common recommendation was to work hard for an extended period of time, and eventually things would work in my favor. You have probably received this generic "work hard" career advancement advice before. It seemed foolproof because most parents tell their children that hard work pays off, so I took it. With that sound advice in hand, I created a basic formula and resolved to do everything my boss asked, outwork everyone around me, and keep a singular focus on high performance. Guess what? It worked, and I quickly emerged as the top salesperson in my organization.

The company was growing, and the director of sales told me he needed to hire another manager. That was exciting news, and all my coworkers knew I would get the job because I was the top performer *and* the hardest worker in the organization. It seemed like the perfect fit.

My Uncomfortable Wake-Up Call

I got into the office early one day, and when I opened the door, I was greeted by the awakening aroma of fresh coffee wafting from the break room. I poured my cup and made small talk with Gordon, an older coworker with perfectly coiffed white hair who resembled former president Clinton.

"They should be announcing that new manager position real soon," he said.

"Yeah, I was thinking the same thing, Gordon."

"Well, you are a pretty sharp young man, Al. I think you would do a great job in that role," he replied. Gordon's wisdom was music to my ears. This was not his first rodeo, so I placed a lot of value in his observation.

Early that afternoon the director of sales called an impromptu department meeting. As we walked to the meeting, my coworkers were looking at me and smiling in anticipation of my good news. The new manager position was the lone agenda item. The director got right to the point and asked everyone to help him congratulate Samuel Jordan on his promotion to the management team. I don't have to tell you my name is not Samuel. *Wait a minute*, I thought to myself. *What just happened? Was I really just passed over for that promotion?*

I was caught completely off guard, but I forced a stoic, unrevealing look onto my face. If you had been standing next to me, you would have seen me smile, join in the collective applause, and congratulate Samuel, who was a close friend of mine. I felt all eighty of my coworkers' eyes focus squarely on me.

Have you ever been the reluctant center of attention? You know how uncomfortable that feels. I had to play it cool because Mama always said, "Never let 'em see you sweat." But deep inside I felt as if I had just been punched in the gut by the winner of the World's Strongest Man competition. I was devastated and confused. My wonderful career plan had turned out to be a dud.

My Search for a Solution

Getting passed over for a promotion has an uncanny way of shaking one's confidence. I called everything I did into question. Was I ineffective? Could my performance improve? Did my boss lack confidence in my potential? These questions forced me to seek out mentors, read countless books, use trial and error to apply every sensible strategy I encountered, and solicit feedback from every source imaginable. Professional development became my part-time job. Have you ever been so focused on something that you could practically taste it? My focus intensified, and I made a commitment to my future because I knew I had talent.

There were a few obvious weaknesses that I needed to address. First, I did not have a clue about how to grow my career within a company, and I was doing so many things the wrong way. My mentors pointed out silly mistakes, and I stumbled across some of them as well. I went back "into the lab" and resolved that I would improve in every possible way. If a strategy or approach did not work, I made adjustments and tried again.

Eventually, things began to fall into place. I left that small marketing firm and joined a major Fortune 100 company that presented new and exciting opportunities. It was time for me to put my research to work with a new approach that required determination and patience. After a while things started to pick up, and I received more opportunities at work. Then I got my first promotion. More great opportunities followed, and I got promoted again. Over the last six years I've received multiple promotions and worked on major organization-wide initiatives, and I am now regarded as a valuable asset to the organization. By the way, that all happened without my having a college degree.

When I decided to write a book about my experience, I wanted to make sure it was a solid project based on facts. This project, a labor of love, started more than two years ago with three critical areas of research. First, I surveyed roughly 750 young professionals from around the country to identify the strategies that are working right now. (What good is it to have old-school strategies for a new-school opportunity?) Second, I interviewed a select group of high-performing gen X and millennial professionals to capture their first-hand experiences. Some of these professionals were honored in "40 under 40" lists of high-performing professionals by the local affiliates of the American City Business Journals. Others represent the best of the best within their companies and generation. Third, I conducted scholarly research to substantiate many of the strategies and principles you will find throughout the text. My practical experience in corporate training, employee development, and leadership development gives me a unique perspective on the most relevant and effective strategies in the marketplace. My personal experience, comprehensive research, and professional expertise all led me to this point. This book and all of its strategies is the culmination of a project that I hope will add value to your career and life.

The Gen X and Millennial Guide to a Thriving Career is intended to be the career-advancement guide that was never taught in college. Universities do a great job of showing graduates how to get a job by stressing résumé-writing, professional attire, interviewing techniques, and other job-search best practices. You attended those workshops at your college or university during your senior year, right? They were probably a good use of your time because the skills you learned helped you land your first job. I don't question the usefulness of those job-prep initiatives; they certainly serve a purpose because many graduates find their first jobs using them. But getting a job is only the first step to establishing a career.

Let's be honest; at some point every professional will come face-to-face with the following question: How do I get promoted and build a healthy and happy career? Too many professionals have the wrong answer or no answer at all. How would you answer the question? I know how it feels to cling to the wrong answer, and the wrong answer causes too many professionals to waste precious time. Competent professionals miss out on promotions every day, but that does not have to be your fate. This book will shorten your learning curve and get you closer to promotion and a career that makes you proud, successful, and happy.

Not Your Father's Corporate America

The workforce has changed significantly over the last decade, and it will change by an even greater degree over the next one. Every day ten thousand baby boomers reach retirement age. The Great Recession will slow the rate of boomer retirements but it will not prevent them, and the baby boomers will continue to retire at an increasing rate. This change is significant because they have owned the corporate world for so long; they dominate senior management and executive positions in both government and private organizations. What will happen when they all begin to retire? Governments and corporate entities won't come to a halt; younger professionals will backfill those positions, and life will go on. The departure of the boomers will create a shock wave of organic opportunity for both generation X and the millennials.

By 2015, the sixty-five-and-over population will grow at a faster rate than the twenty-to-sixty-four age group (US Bureau of Labor Statistics 2013). What will be the implications for the workforce? Senior managers will become executives, middle managers will become senior managers, front-line managers will become middle managers, and front-line or entry-level employees will become front-line managers. While my portrayal of the coming advancement opportunities may be overly simplistic, the most important thing to understand is that change is upon us. How will you fit into this workplace transformation? You will either be a spectator or a participant. Professionals who understand strategic career advancement will seize this opportunity.

A Practical Solution

Every professional dreads a dead-end career, but too few of us know how to resuscitate one. This book is all about solutions.

A powerful strategy emerged after I surveyed and interviewed about 750 professionals from around the country. I have always believed that if you want to be good at something, go find a person who is successful in that area and do what he or she has done. Seems pretty practical, right? I have a bias against unnecessarily reinventing the wheel, and wasting time annoys me. The good news is that the data point to a sound career-advancement strategy that I have synthesized into what I call my Differentiation Model.

The model is built upon three central principles:

- High performers always find ways to add significant value to their organizations, so they are viewed as critical assets that must be developed.
- It is not enough to just be valuable. A common characteristic of upwardly mobile professionals is their ability to differentiate themselves consistently from their peers. They have a sophisticated ability to create a stark contrast between themselves and everyone around them.
- The "secret sauce" lies in the combination of the first two points to create differentiated value. Professionals who find the right mix of value and differentiation are promoted

faster than their peers and are assigned the most visible and important projects—projects that lead to a thriving career.

This solution is as simple as it is effective. Along with many young professionals, I have implemented this strategy and found success. Those who find ways to be valuable and different increase their likelihood of securing a thriving career.

A Targeted Approach

Any sound strategy requires a specific set of behaviors for optimal execution, and this model is no different. I would never advise someone to do things differently just for the sake of being different. If you owned a hotdog stand, it would not make sense to ditch hotdog buns and use hamburger buns for no apparent reason. Your customers would think you were crazy, stupid, or both, and that will lead you nowhere.

The goal is to identify valuable behaviors and to differentiate yourself without sacrificing value in order to maximize the impact of your efforts. This book outlines seven competencies that, when implemented, offer value to your organization and differentiation to you.

- Perform consistently.
- Communicate effectively.
- Build two-way relationships.
- Be a change champion.
- Study your craft.

- Advertise your ambition.
- Be a professional.

You Might Find What You've Been Looking For

This book is meant to be a resource and a guide, not a novel, so you certainly do not have to read it in order. Feel free to take a prescriptive approach and start with the chapter that is most beneficial to your circumstances.

Each chapter has practical advice that is drawn directly from my survey research, interviews, and personal experiences. Technically, this is a how-to book. I have often been frustrated by such books that are heavy on the "what" and light on the "how," so my goal is to give you as much "how" as this format will allow. At the end of each chapter, you will find a number of resources with which you can continue your learning.

At the end of the day, our careers represent more than just a paycheck. What we do for a living plays a huge role in who we are and in our overall self-image. Dead-end jobs and careers deflate our ambition and cause us to wonder where everything went wrong. Have you ever had a job you hated? Did it affect your ability to be happy in other areas of your life? I don't know whether the deep connection to our work is healthy, but it can't be ignored.

Treat this book like your personal career-advancement journal. Congratulations on taking the first step toward a thriving career. Enjoy the journey!

CHAPTER 1

THE NEW NORMAL

If you ask ten people for their perspective on how to get promoted, you will probably get ten different answers. The most common answer will more than likely be a generic "just do your job well," followed by a confused "I don't know." Those responses do not provide much clarity. Many professionals have implemented a trial-and-error approach or outdated approaches to getting more from the workplace. Neither option yields the best results.

Happy Careers = Happy Employees

This statement is going to shock you: Employees with promising careers are happier than employees who do not see a path to career growth. Not really breaking news, is it? In 2009, 76 percent of respondents said career advancement is important or very important to job satisfaction (US Bureau of Labor Statistics 2009). This staggering statistic leads to the question, why is career advancement so important to us?

I often say a career is not community service. Community service is something we do for others, while pursuing a thriving career is something we do for ourselves. Does that sound selfish? The pursuit of a career does have a selfish element, but there is absolutely nothing wrong with that. We do not go to work every day without expecting adequate compensation. Our time, effort, and passion are not free. We must get something of value out of our work experience.

What would you do if your boss called and said your company would be withholding your salary but would still expect you to report to work? Would you go to work or start updating your résumé? The bottom line is we want to be paid so we can make a living. The more promising your career, the better chance you have to draw the salary that will support your desired standard of living.

A good salary is one of the many reasons that we wake up every morning and trek to the office. Here is a list of the most common reasons that my survey respondents said they go to work every day:

- earn a good salary
- enjoy the work
- support my family
- enjoy challenges
- sense of accomplishment
- establish college funds
- living my passion
- like my coworkers
- need the benefits
- don't want to sit at home

Why do you go to work every day? Are your reasons listed above? Circle all of the reasons that motivate you to get up early, battle traffic, and deal with your least favorite coworkers. If you have other reasons that did not make the list, write them next to my list. It is important to understand and acknowledge the value that a thriving career brings to your life as you read this book.

It is obvious that our careers do a lot for us. That is why it is so troubling to see 45 percent of survey respondents say they are only somewhat satisfied with their careers (US Bureau of Labor Statistics 2009). I always wonder about the adverse impact that an unfulfilling career can have on other parts of a person's life. What impact does an unfulfilling job or poor career outlook have on your personal happiness? How does it affect relationships with your significant other, your children, and your friends? I don't want to paint a gloomy picture, but it is important to be honest about the downside of an impotent career.

I remember when I first left Bradley University in 2003 and relocated to Charlotte, North Carolina, because I ran out of money. You may know people who have faced the same set of circumstances. College is expensive, so this is an all-too-common reality for thousands of students every year. With my incomplete college career behind me, it was time to venture into the adult world of jobs, bills, and responsibilities. Starting a career is tough, but it's even more complicated when you don't have a bachelor's degree.

The first two years in Charlotte were very difficult for me. My friends from college graduated and began promising careers, while I struggled to find the right prescription to heal my sick career prospects. It became difficult for me to talk to my friends about

3

their successes when I couldn't contribute to the conversation. Don't get me wrong: I was happy for them, but my own career accomplishments remained elusive. I used to be ashamed of my lack of progress. Especially considering that I knew I had a lot of unrealized potential. There were important needs in my life that were unfulfilled. I wanted to do something meaningful, earn a decent salary, establish some savings, and find a robust intellectual challenge. All of these things could have been satisfied by a productive career.

A deficient career can cause anyone to question his or her ability to do great work. I often wondered whether I would ever pull it all together. That uncertainty dogged me. I am a fairly intelligent guy with a solid work ethic but did not have much to show for it.

Finally, after a lot of hard work and persistence, things began to fall into place for me. I stumbled upon a sales career that slowly gained traction. Talking has always been pretty easy for me. (My brother Chris always told me I'd end up doing something that allowed me to talk because I never let him get a word in. I guess he was right.) It was a liberating feeling.

As my career improved, so did other parts of my life. I was able to reconnect with friends and share my stories of progress and success. In addition, I was able to finally complete my bachelor's degree 5 months prior to the printing of this book.

How does your career affect your life? Is your behavior different outside the office when you are unhappy in the office? This is an important question to consider as you read this book.

Things Have Changed

The baby boomers used to control everything. Boomers, born between 1946 and 1964, total 80 million people, and the sheer size of the generation made them an important force. They developed a reputation for being hard-working professionals who lived to work and did not care about work-life balance. The boomer perspective on career management has been the rule because they have been at the helm of the corporate ship. A large part of the workforce, they hold senior positions across all segments of the corporate world.

In 2010 this generation began to hit retirement age at a rate of 3,800 people per day, and by 2020 the rate will almost triple (US Bureau of Labor Statistics 2013). The Great Recession's impact on retirement accounts caused a number of boomers to delay their golden years of relaxation, but this massive exodus from the workforce is still inevitable. The baby boomer generation will eventually retire, and the country will need competent, capable professionals to fill the massive void they leave behind.

The workforce is expected to grow by 10.4 million workers between 2010 and 2020. While the number of workers aged 16–24 will decrease by 2.6 million, the number aged 25–54 will increase by 1.6 million, and the number aged 55 and older will increase by 11.5 million (US Bureau of Labor Statistics 2012). We don't need to worry about a shrinking workforce; the concern is the aging-out of the most experienced group in our workforce. What cohort of professionals is ready to backfill the boomers' roles at the top of the corporate world? Generation X (1965–1980) and millennial (1981–2000) professionals have to pay close attention to the impact of the boomer retirements on the workforce they will inherit. How will the rest of the workforce respond? What are the key issues to consider during the demographic transition? How will this impact future personnel decisions? These are all important questions with which serious gen X and millennial professionals must grapple.

Thriving careers aren't created in a vacuum but exist within the realities of the current workforce. Some professionals will choose a reactive response to the pending workforce changes and wander aimlessly from opportunity to opportunity without a coherent strategy. I wouldn't have written this book if I thought that was an effective approach. Professionals who make the decision to manage their careers proactively and strategically in this new environment are the ones who will ultimately win.

Knowledge Gaps

Many organizations learned to rely on the impressive skill and performance of the boomer generation. This relationship grew closer as the boomers displayed an intense sense of loyalty and commitment to their employers. Many boomers don't understand the idea of switching companies every four to five years, and it is not difficult to find boomers who have worked for one company for their entire professional careers. My in-laws each worked more than 25 years with the same company. This deep sense of loyalty to a company is a hallmark of the boomer generation. Their long relationships with their employers allowed the boomers to learn a great deal about the human, social, cultural, and structural components of their companies, information that allowed them to perform at high levels in their roles for a long time. The depth of their experience allowed them to identify cross-functional synergies in their work and increase productivity.

If you were the CEO of a company, would you find value in an employee base that understood the ins and outs of your organization? Do you think that would help you reach your strategic goals? I certainly can't see a problem with such a scenario. Many companies have taken the boomers' loyalty and experience for granted. So what happens to that wealth of information—and loyalty—when the boomers retire?

Many companies, particularly industrial ones, see the loss of deep organizational intelligence (Harrison 2008) as a significant organizational development challenge. Employees need to explain the company's culture, unwritten rules, and organizational structure. These are critical roles that can't go unfilled. Organizations now have a competitive imperative to transfer this knowledge to younger employees. Someone has to confidently guide departments, business units, and divisions as they execute company strategy.

A 2006 Knowledge Infusion survey collected responses from nearly four hundred human resources professionals from both small and large enterprises, revealing that over 50 percent of the respondents knew that the retiring workforce will cause a knowledge and skill gap, but less than 30 percent of them had a formally prepared, viable retention plan (Harrison 2008). A number of knowledge-retention strategies have been deployed throughout the corporate landscape. Some of the more common strategies involve comprehensive talent-succession planning, mentoring programs with experienced staff and young high-potential employees, and flexible work options like telecommuting and part-time schedules for boomers.

Companies everywhere continue to take steps to hedge against the boomers' retirement, and this workforce change provides an extraordinary opportunity for the right person. You can be the right person. Great things happen when preparation meets opportunity. You can use this book as a tool to jumpstart the preparation process.

The Talent Vacuum

It is time for the younger employees to step up. Organizations are in the process of activating their succession plans to identify professionals who are ready for their next assignment. Executives will move into C-level positions, middle managers will join the executive ranks, and first-level leaders will become middle managers. Of course, I made that transition sound neat, orderly, and seamless, but things don't always happen that way in the workplace. The more important point is that there will be organic organizational movement, and the next generation of leaders has an opportunity to fill the talent void caused by boomers' retirements.

Gen X, with 40 million members, is dwarfed by the 80 million boomers. Millennials account for 72 million Americans, but many are still in the very early stages of their careers. This means gen X and high-potential millennials must answer the call, creating an amazing opportunity for the young professional. Timing is everything, and there could not be a better time to be in the workforce than now.

We are still recovering from the Great Recession, but it is only a matter of time until everything returns to normal. Will you be ready to capitalize on the wide array of advancement opportunities as the workplace demographics change? Be honest with yourself when you answer that question. The prepared professional has an opportunity to thrive, but the unprepared employee's lack of preparation is a meager down payment on an unfulfilling career.

Before we continue, let me add a disclaimer: Members of a generation share some characteristics because of the similar societal environments in which they are raised. However, generational characteristics are not absolute.

For example, I am a member of the millennial generation, but I share many values with baby boomers. As you read the following generational summaries, remember that some of the characteristics may not perfectly match your individual behavior or values, but these generalities reasonably describe the most common traits of each generation. This information is based on the highly reputable work of Lynne C. Lancaster and David Stillman, authors of *When Generations Collide at Work* (2002) and *The M-Factor* (2010). Taken together, these books offer a comprehensive analysis of the workplace traits of the baby boomers, generation X, and the millennials.

Who Is Generation X?

Generation X, those born between 1961 and 1980, number roughly 40 million members. This group is defined by their childhood experience as latchkey kids. Increased divorce rates and working mothers caused this group to find themselves home alone, fending for themselves. They did their homework alone and cooked their own dinners. They navigated their adolescent years with minimal supervision. Generation X's unique set of characteristics can be traced back to the structure of their childhood.

Work Values

Pragmatic and practical in their approach to work, gen X wants to eliminate the task. Self-reliance and independence, two critically important values to gen Xers, stem from their experience as latchkey kids. They have been independent all their lives and are easily frustrated by work environments that don't provide independence. Gen X also appreciates a laid-back work environment. They appreciate simple structure but detest excessive structure and hierarchy. The flat organizational structure with reduced levels of hierarchy that has gained popularity in recent years is no coincidence, considering that many gen X members are moving into prominent organizational leadership positions.

Communication Style

Gen Xers value direct and immediate communication and don't like the organizational structure that leads to nuanced, political communication. They place tremendous value on task execution, and direct communication complements that strategy. Pragmatism is critical to a strong workplace experience, and gen X says what they mean and mean what they say. (Sometimes this approach rubs boomers the wrong way because they tend to appreciate hierarchy and apply it to their communication style.) Gen X also values immediate feedback on their performance, which is attributed to their task-oriented sense of urgency about getting their work done and receiving feedback.

Work and Family Life

Baby boomers live to work, so their careers are paramount, and they work entirely too much. Gen X had parents who missed too many dance recitals and basketball games, and they realize that too much career loyalty can adversely impact family life. Therefore, gen Xers work to live, not the other way around; work is a tool that allows them to live better, more fulfilling lives. Work-life balance became increasingly popular as this generation grew in the workplace, and flexibility and freedom became the best way to reward good performance. Work-life balance is a nonnegotiable right, so it is common for a gen Xer to ask for more vacation days during salary negotiations for a new job, while boomers would ask for higher pay.

Career Expectations

For gen X a career is not a one-stop proposition; it is a journey with multiple stops along the way, each providing a different area of skill development and experience. Gen X wants a portable career.

Gen X rose in the workforce during the proliferation of leadership-development programs. Jack Welch pioneered this strategy during his tenure at General Electric, rotating his high-performing leaders through different business units in order to provide them with a diverse set of skills and giving himself the flexibility to plug a strong leader into any area and see success. Gen X built upon this strategy, seeing little benefit in a one-company career. They saw their parents laid-off and dealing with job insecurity, so they expect to work for multiple companies over the course of a career. This doesn't mean they aren't loyal. Gen X members work hard and are loyal to their work and team. They just aren't willing to commit to a company for a lifetime. It is important to them to keep their options open so they aren't casualties of corporate downsizing and restructuring. They've seen that movie, and it gave them nightmares!

Who Are the Millennials?

The millennials, born between 1981 and 2000, are a massive generation of approximately 72 million members whose parents are both the boomers and gen X. Millennials were the beneficiaries of significant parental involvement. Baby boomers and gen X became involved in their millennial children's lives because they did not want to replicate the gen X childhood experience and raise another group of latchkey kids. Therefore, the boomers resolved to become close advisors to their millennial children and guide them through every aspect of life, while gen X parents wanted to be the parents they never had growing up. Thus, millennial children received more than enough support and advice throughout their formative years. Millennials also lived through significant periods of technological change and economic prosperity, and all of this support, feedback, and positive reinforcement manifests itself in the workplace.

Work Values

Millennials always look for the next big accomplishment and always ask what is next. This trait can be both a healthy and an unhealthy impatience. Some tasks require time, but millennials tend to appreciate and expect instant gratification, a perspective that makes them great multitaskers who can handle multiple priorities. The group is goal-oriented and tenacious in the pursuit of those goals. Work is not just "nine to five"; it has to have meaning and be valuable. Millennials need to do things that have a purpose, as work is not what they do; it is who they are. Any conflict between their values and their work must be addressed, or they will find another job. This need for meaning is explained by the increased focus on volunteerism during their childhood, as college admissions professionals began to place a greater emphasis on organizational involvement and community service as this generation came of age. Therefore, millennials developed an appreciation for altruism at an early age. This group is also innovative and entrepreneurial, and their search for meaning allows them to bring a unique perspective to their work.

Communication Style

Technology is king, and this group prefers to communicate via text, email, voicemail, or interoffice instant messenger. Fast communication is more important than face-to-face communication. The technological revolution sped up many areas of human life, and communication is one of them. Face-to-face communication—even voice communication—is antiquated and unnecessary. This group doesn't diminish the value of communication—it is actually critically important to them—but they communicate differently from any generation before them.

Millennials also expect constant feedback. Their constant need to know that they are doing things the right way is a nuisance to gen X because that group values independence. But don't blame the millennials, blame their parents. Remember they are accustomed to significant parental involvement, and a great deal of that parental involvement came in the form of feedback. Millennials value their parental feedback, and they expect it to continue in the workplace.

Work and Family Life

Work-life balance is very important to millennials, who, like gen X, work to live, not the other way around. They don't want to be married to their work, even though it has meaning, so flexibility in the workplace is critical. They enjoy the idea of telecommuting and virtual work. Balance is an expectation; millennials won't be married to their jobs.

Career Expectations

Millennials will ask how to become the CEO of their company during the interview. This is an ambitious group; they want success, and they want it yesterday. They laugh at the idea of working with one company for a majority of their career. Since their careers fund their lives, they want to get as far as possible in the shortest amount of time. Again, you can't blame them; they were born into a dynamic technological age that has yet to slow down. If they have a question about something, they just Google it. If they want to buy a book, they pull out their smartphones and download the ebook. Everything happens fast.

Millennials also expect the most qualified person to get the best opportunities and struggle to understand why they may be passed over for a promotion if they are qualified. Their pursuit of high performance is their default way of advancing their careers. Millennials are not loyal to companies; they are loyal to people.

The New Approach

Things are certainly changing, but not everyone knows it. Too many professionals will wander about the workplace without understanding the new rules. That is like deciding to play a game of cricket when you don't know the first rule of the game. There's a good chance you won't be a good teammate or a strong performer.

The boomers once were able to define the best approach because they were the only game in town, but their rules don't fit the new workforce that is dominated by gen X and millennials. Boomers believed if they stayed with one company, worked hard, and made work their priority, eventually their big break would come when they were "next in line." Contrast that idea with the gen X and millennial desire for work-life balance and willingness to jump from company to company in pursuit of a meaningful career. The dominant generation gets to set the rules because they make the personnel decisions, and gen X and the millennials will dominate the workforce of the future. We are in the beginning stages of the transition right now. The rules are already changing.

Unfortunately, many young professionals will continue to behave according to an outdated rulebook. They will miss out on opportunities and never understand why. There is no need for anyone to walk down that road. There is a better, more effective option available. Are you open to a new strategy? Do you find value in a thriving career? If so, you need to keep reading to learn about this new set of rules.

The new approach supports the opportunistic professional, the individual who values differentiation and understands the value of their performance. This new approach is simple yet effective. Many professionals have already begun to pursue this strategy, and it is working. They treat their careers as their personal brands. Since the new rules suggest their careers evolve as their brand strengthens, they look for ways to add to their professional "product"—themselves—every day.

CHAPTER 2

THE DIFFERENTIATION MODEL

"You must be willing to do the things that others won't do today, in order to have the things that others don't have tomorrow."
—Les Brown, motivational speaker

Did you ever play the Where's Waldo game when you were a kid? I certainly did. Unfortunately, I never found Waldo, although it seemed as if everyone else eventually found him. My lack of success became so frustrating that eventually I didn't even want to attempt to find Waldo because I just knew my date with failure was certain. Why did the game have to be so difficult? (Come to think of it, I may need to lie down on someone's couch and talk about how Waldo scarred me for life.) Maybe you had better luck than I did. Did you ever find Waldo?

I always wondered why I could not find him, but apparently, I am not the only one to ponder this question. Robert Desimone, director of the McGovern Institute for Brain Research at MIT, and his colleagues at the National Institute of Health set out to determine how the brain works to find Waldo. The study addresses the central question of whether the brain engages in serial processing, which scans like a mental spotlight moving across a dark page, or parallel processing, which takes in the whole page at once and gradually zooms in on relevant features like color and shape (Neuroscience Institute 2005). The study basically reveals how the brain recognizes and processes differences.

Desimone recorded the eye movements and activity of specific neurons in macaque monkeys while the monkeys scanned a complex array in an experimental equivalent of looking for Waldo. Desimone focused on neurons that belong to the V4 area, a midregion of the visual cortex known to be important to attention. Someone found a way to give a group of monkeys the legendary Where's Waldo experience!

Neurons have areas of specialization. For example, some neurons specialize in color recognition while others specialize in recognizing shapes. When a neuron with a "blue" color specialty observes the color blue in Waldo's shirt, it begins to fire signals to the brain that communicate that the eyes are viewing a blue object. It is the equivalent of someone yelling, "Hey, buddy! Look over here!" But how can a neuron be heard over all the other neurons that are battling for the brain's attention? The study concluded that the neurons are finally "heard" when they synchronize their signals. Think of the last time you attended a professional basketball game. It was so loud you couldn't hear the conversations between fans five rows in front or behind you, right? However, when everyone in the arena began to chant, "*De*-fense! *De*-fense!" it was easy to hear what was being said. That is what neurons do to draw your attention to Waldo. They scream in unison, which makes it easier for you to focus on images that resemble Waldo's shape, colors, and size.

The difficulty in finding Waldo comes when the blue, red, and white neurons in the visual cortex struggle to get in sync when many other objects share Waldo's colors. The game would be easier if Waldo's shirt contained colors that were different from the background colors of the scene because it would be easier for the neurons to synchronize their communication. The bottom line is that the brain employs a consistent process to recognize differences.

Even with this new knowledge, I still can't find Waldo.

The most interesting part of this research is not *how* we recognize differences but our need *to* recognize differences. Differences matter to humans. We place a huge emphasis on identifying differences across almost all areas of life in order to make effective decisions.

- If you are alone at a social gathering, you may scan the room to find the most attractive person to approach and engage in conversation. Differences matter in romantic and social relationships.
- When I was a child, I always wanted to snag the biggest piece of meatloaf off the plate or the largest portion of spaghetti Look, as the youngest of five children, I needed to be able to reconcile those differences in size quickly and take action! Differences are important to our survival.
- Hiring managers and human resources professionals comb résumés, interview results, and LinkedIn profiles to determine the best candidate for a job opening. They

must reconcile the differences among all candidates before they extend an offer for employment. Differences are an important factor in employment decisions.

How can we apply this understanding to career-advancement strategies? Hold that thought as we continue to explore the importance of differentiation.

Lessons from *Sesame Street*

Sesame Street was a fixture in my household when I was growing up. Big Bird, Bert, and Ernie were the coolest cast of characters around. One of my favorite *Sesame Street* segments was the one in which they compared and contrasted objects. Big Bird would saunter onto the set, display three or four items, and then start singing his song about how one of the things is not like the other.

I didn't know it then, but this exercise triggered activity in the visual cortex region of the brain. The activity is a learning tool that helps children recognize patterns and differences. The *Sesame Street* creators developed this iconic segment because it helps children develop a critical skill that they will use forever.

All of this *Sesame Street* talk has me feeling a bit nostalgic. Complete the two sample activities below. You know the rules: identify the item that does not belong in the group, but also note how long it takes you to identify the misplaced item in each group.

Activity A

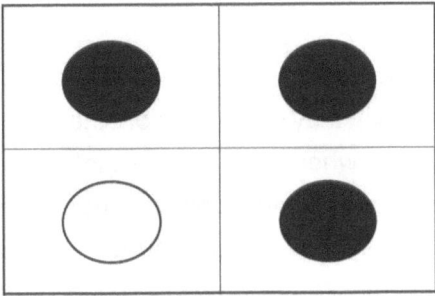

Activity B

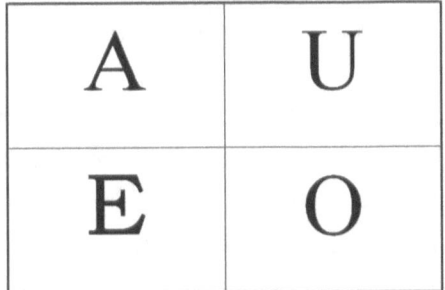

Let's take a moment to discuss each activity. The answer to both activities is the bottom-left square. Which did you complete in the shortest amount of time? Most people finish Activity A first because there is a high degree of contrast between the three similar objects and the "not like the others" one. Three ovals are shaded and one is not. Chances are it took you less than two seconds to identify the unshaded oval. More contrast leads to a greater visibility. Activity B takes most people longer to complete because there is a low degree of contrast with the differences. Letters A, U, and O are in the Times New Roman font, while letter E is in the Bookman Old Style font. Because the two fonts have similar characteristics, you probably took more time to identify the misplaced item. You may even have given up because it was too challenging.

Our brain wants to recognize differences, and things become more noticeable when they stand out from the crowd. Things stand out from the crowd when they have a high degree of contrast or differentiation. Pretty simple concept, right? If you want to be noticed, you must emphasize how you are different from others. How easy would the Where's Waldo game be if Waldo had a Mohawk and wore a hot pink shirt?

Differences Matter in the Workplace

Organizations discuss differences all the time. You can't watch thirty minutes of television without being bombarded by advertisements and sales pitches that highlight how Company A is superior to Company B. The relentless focus on the differences among products and services in the marketplace is all part of an attempt to define a company's competitive advantage.

What is your competitive advantage as an employee? Corporate leaders are conditioned to appreciate and reward differences that add value. The concept of differentiation is a major decision-making lever used by organizational leaders, hiring managers, and human resources professionals. Consider the following example and the importance of differentiation:

Imagine you've just become the CEO of Hotdogs 'R' Us. The company is a national gourmet hotdog cart franchise that is set to expand its operations in California. You need to decide between two marketing proposals and identify the best plan to increase sales. The first proposal outlines how Hotdogs 'R' Us has more locations, higher-quality food, faster service, and cheaper prices than all of its California-based competitors. This proposal focuses on the differences between Hotdogs 'R' Us and its competitors. The second proposal takes a different approach and outlines the similarities between the company and its competitors. It documents how Hotdogs 'R' Us is as big as, as fast as, and as cheap as all of its competitors. Which proposal do you choose? Which proposal presents the best case to potential customers to visit your hotdog stand?

The first proposal is the only one worth consideration. Customers want to know how your product is different from the other guy's product down the street. We like to buy products that give us something different, whether a better price, higher quality, or better service.

I have been in sales for nearly ten years. I have sold many products and facilitated too many sales training sessions to count. Every salesperson is taught to emphasize the differences in their product's quality, features, and cost in order to position their product as the best option. Customers expect a salesperson to explain a product's competitive advantage so they can make an informed buying decision.

The decision-making process for a hiring manager is similar to that of the single person at a social gathering looking for a date and a hungry child during dinner who wants the most appealing plate. They think through all the points of differentiation and then make a decision.

The Differentiation Model Explained

Differences matter. Companies and customers, managers and employees all pay attention to differences. What differences define your brand in the workplace? How are you different from your coworkers? You are the chairman and CEO of You, Inc. You are the product. Your company is your customer. What is your competitive advantage? What value proposition do you provide to your employer? The professionals who offer the most compelling value proposition to their companies are uniquely positioned to capitalize on the pending shift in workplace demographics. A thriving career awaits those with the best competitive advantage.

Every professional must provide value to his or her company. The value you bring to your company is the justification for your employment, compensation, and benefits. When considering this value conversation, I find it useful to simplify the idea in this way: you must create more value than you capture. People who don't add value to their organizations typically have uneventful and stagnant careers. You can't be one of these people if you want to have upward mobility and a thriving career.

Keep in mind that valuable contributions vary from professional to professional, so your specific job function and your company's overall strategy determine the actions and behaviors that your company considers valuable. A department manager adds value differently from an entry-level business analyst, and a senior executive adds value differently from a change-management consultant. You know you add a *basic* level of value to your organization if you consistently and effectively achieve the tasks listed in your job description. But how can you add more value?

24

The most successful gen X and millennial professionals do a great job of identifying how they can add value to their organizations, but doing a good job is not enough. That strategy worked well for the baby boomers, but things are different now. For example, think of a coworker or friend who is great at his or her job, has solid performance, and yet is passed over for promotion after promotion. Why doesn't your friend or coworker get opportunities when he or she does great work?

The Waldo Effect

Your friend is a victim of the Waldo Effect. Remember why it is difficult to find Waldo? It is because there is only a small contrast between Waldo and the scenes in which he is placed. The colors of his clothing and the shape of his body are similar to everything around him, and the result is that you can't find him. Professionals who only do great work and nothing else render their efforts all but invisible. Personnel decision makers don't think of them when making promotion decisions, so they remain in their roles while frustration mounts. Remember organizational leaders are wired to notice differences because doing so is a key competency in those who hold positions at that level.

Professionals in this category do a great job and want to grow their careers, but one thing they are missing is a complete body of work. I am all too familiar with the Waldo Effect. The first time I was passed over for a promotion, I was a great salesperson, but nothing else. I had an incomplete body of work. Unfortunately, I had to learn this lesson the hard way and endure the sting of disappointment. I had figured all I had to do was work hard and perform well. That silver bullet worked for the boomers, but it does not work anymore.

The Sesame Street *Effect*

Adding value is not enough. Today's high-performing professionals take their performance to the next level and add differentiated value. I call this the *Sesame Street* Effect. Yes, it is an unconventional name, but it actually makes sense. Remember why it was easier to identify the nonshaded oval in the first activity earlier in this chapter than it was to identify the difference in the fonts in the second activity? There was a high degree of contrast between each object, which made the differences stand out. Differentiated value has the same effect in the workplace. This is human nature: we pay more attention to what is different and stands out. Why not harness the predictable tendencies of human nature to create a thriving career?

Professionals who get those promotions and opportunities strategically add value in areas that offer high visibility and differentiation. They don't just want to make it easy for organizational leaders to notice them; they want to add value that makes it almost impossible to be ignored. So how do they do this? What steps do they take?

Ask yourself two questions as you approach your work. First, how can I add significant value? Remember value looks different based on your role, your department, and the company's overall strategy. This question is the first question because your efforts have to mean something. You can't be different for the sake of being different; that doesn't accomplish anything. Activity that does not add value is a waste of time. Value identification is paramount.

After you identify what actions and behaviors are valuable, you can determine how to display those behaviors differently from your counterparts. The most successful professionals do a great job of accentuating the ways they add value to their organizations in ways that look different for each person.

How Do You Measure Up?

Differentiation Quadrants

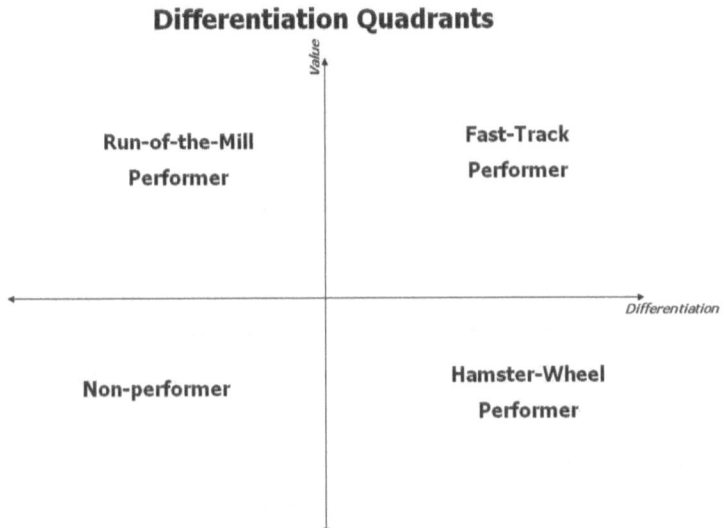

Having explained the thought process behind my Differentiation Model, now I want to give you an opportunity to determine how you measure up against it. The differentiation quadrants add an additional layer of clarity to the concept. The x-axis reflects the amount of differentiation a professional exhibits while executing his or her responsibilities, while the y-axis reflects the level of value the professional delivers within his or her job function. Below you will find a description of the typical professional who resides in each quadrant. At the end of the quadrant descriptions, try to identify the quadrant in which you belong.

The Nonperformer

This is the **low differentiation/low value** quadrant. People who fall into this quadrant will not have long careers with their organizations, as they are often the targets of performance management and disciplinary processes. They do not produce valuable work. There is a good chance that they are in roles that are poor fits for their skills.

Hamster-Wheel Performer

This is the **high differentiation/low value** quadrant. Those who fall into this quadrant are the personification of creativity. They are always trying to figure out how to do things differently. They hate the status quo and love times of organizational change. Unfortunately, they are focused on being different without purpose, and they struggle to add value in their roles. They have potential that can be tapped if they are under the right leadership, but they may be labeled as people who have great ideas and poor execution. Hamster-wheel performers generate a significant amount of activity, but their efforts rarely result in meaningful achievements.

Run-of-the-Mill Performer

This is the **low differentiation/high value** quadrant. A majority of professionals live here. They do high-quality work, but it is done under the radar. They do everything requested of them and make it easy for organizational leaders to take them for granted. These are the professionals who become frustrated because they add a considerable amount of value to their organization, but it seems as though no one pays attention. They tend to be pigeon-holed into particular roles and stay there. Run-of-the-mill performers are ready, willing, and able to expand their responsibilities, but they have a weak brand, despite their competence.

Fast-Track Performer

This is the **high differentiation/high value** quadrant. Those who fall into this quadrant are on the fast track, everything they touch turns into gold, and they get all of the opportunities to work on the most high-profile and high-impact assignments. Fast-track performers do great work, they do it better than their counterparts, and everyone in the office knows it. They have been promoted multiple times and have strong career trajectories. They set the standard for today's professionals, work hard and smart, and are well positioned to capitalize on the baby boomers' exit from the workforce.

The remainder of the book focuses on the behaviors or competencies of the fast-track performer. Each chapter outlines a different competency and explains how to create a high degree of differentiation with it. I identified these seven critical competencies via extensive survey research, additional scholarly research, and interviews with a group of high-performing professionals from around the country. The competencies are listed in order of importance.

At the beginning of each chapter, you will find my Promotion Pyramid, which captures the hierarchical importance of the competencies. The Promotion Pyramid provides a framework through which you can view and assess the health of your own career.

This book can be a great guide to creating a thriving career. I encourage you to read each chapter and to evaluate honestly where you are on the continuum of effectiveness within each competency. It is difficult to fix a problem you can't see. After all, when was the last time you were able to fix an issue in your life of which you were unaware?

I hope you are ready to evaluate your skills within each competency honestly and to chart a course to improve where necessary. Honest self-reflection is the seed that allows change to grow within your life. I wish you the absolute best as you begin this journey.

CHAPTER 3

PERFORM CONSISTENTLY

"Well done is better than well said."
—Benjamin Franklin, statesman and inventor

Have you ever had to babysit three curious and energetic little girls all at the same time? I was the lucky uncle who got to take care of my three beautiful nieces while my brother Chris ran a few errands. I figured it would be easy; after all, I am the cool uncle whom they affectionately call "Uncle A."

As Chris headed out the door, he said, "Oh, by the way, they need to eat breakfast, so just put something together." Put something together? I had no clue what to make for three hungry little girls. For the first time in my life, cooking breakfast seemed like a Herculean task. It did not help that I'm not exactly a five-star chef. If my food was bad, would I lose my "cool uncle" status?

That was simply unacceptable because the "cool uncle" label comes with perks. My nieces are always happy to see me. They run and tackle me with hugs on a regular basis and always tell me they miss me on phone calls. Who in their right mind would want to give that up?

I pulled myself together and began looking through the cabinets for my options while my nieces watched an episode of *Dora the Explorer*. I was getting nowhere, so I turned to my nieces and asked what they wanted for breakfast. Why did I bother? They all wanted popsicles, but there was no way I could feed them that for breakfast.

I quickly thumbed through my mental rolodex of responsible adult responses and said, "After you eat your grits, you can have a popsicle, okay?" They seemed to like that idea. I grabbed the instant grits and we had a great breakfast.

When Chris got home and saw his daughters' blue popsicle-stained tongues, he was pretty annoyed. I guess that is the price you pay for allowing the cool uncle to babysit your children.

That experience illustrates the most basic career-advancement principle: be a good steward of your current opportunity in order to demonstrate that you deserve another one. This is nothing new. At some point in your childhood, you had a conversation with your parents similar to the one I had with my three nieces; you wanted a cup of ice cream after dinner, and your mom made you finish your green beans first. Maybe you wanted a new bike, but your dad said you must first take care of the bike you have. It looks like mom and dad know best, even when it comes to career advancement.

The first step toward a thriving career is to perform at a high level in your current role. Companies want to grow the careers of professionals who have a strong track record of performance.

The Entry-Level Abyss

Many entry-level positions are bland, limited in scope, or quite repetitive. This can be frustrating because most young professionals have diverse skills that are often underutilized in an entry-level role. Unfortunately, CEO is not a job posting found in the entrylevel section of a career website. However, there is good news: Entry-level positions often lead to management or other rewarding opportunities. Still, the more attractive opportunities will not be an option in your development plan if you don't perform consistently in the entry-level position.

When I started with my company, I knew I could do more. However, my boss did not care much about my potential until he saw strong results in my first role. You may find that to be harsh; managers should care about their employee's aspirations and potential, and the best leaders definitely care about their team member's career goals. However, leaders are required to care most about delivering solid results from their team and department every day, so your leader's primary focus is on the delivery of solid results. His or her secondary focus is your career-development goals. When you demonstrate your ability to perform at a high level and add value in your current role, you make it easier for your leader to focus on your career development. Many people violate this rule and become frustrated when promotions remain elusive.

My fellow millennials are accustomed to speed in every facet of life. Instead of going to a store to buy our favorite artist's album, we download it onto our phones without leaving the house. We live in an on-demand culture, but our career advancement does not always operate within that same paradigm. It is important to create a body of work or career portfolio that your manager can refer to as justification to move you into a new role.

I often compare entry-level positions to that intense finance, calculus, or physics class in a university curriculum that is designed to weed out the pretenders and identify the contenders. Did you have a class like that in your undergraduate or graduate program? You probably noticed that not everyone who started that class finished it. The fast-track performer is able to stay the course, find ways to enhance his or her skills, and perform at a high level in an entry-level job.

Know Thy Job Requirements

Every job has a specific set of responsibilities. Job postings on company websites describe each requirement in great detail, and companies put considerable time and effort into determining the performance expectations for every position. Specific job requirements serve as a roadmap to high performance. Take a look at the two targets in figure 3.1.

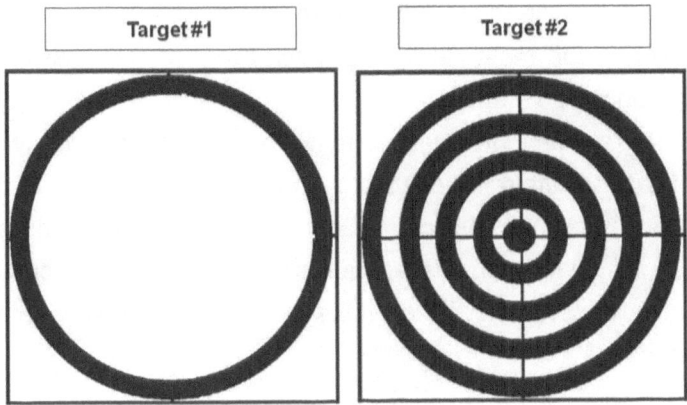

Figure 3.1

Imagine you have just entered a competition to win $50,000 and are competing against another person. You both have to shoot an arrow at one of the targets, and the person whose arrow lands closest to the bull's-eye wins. Since you entered the contest first, you get to choose the target you want to shoot. Keep in mind that both targets are identical in size. Will you choose Target #1 or Target #2?

Naturally, most people choose Target #2 because it is easier to see its bull's-eye. The same principle applies to your job performance. It is easier to perform at a high level when you know what is required. If you never understand your role requirements, you are playing the lottery with your performance and career.

Once you understand your primary responsibilities, make sure you focus on them every day. This is the practice of keeping the main thing the main thing. Distractions will come, but the fast-track performer always stays focused on the most important tasks.

There is one role in my office where high-quality performance coaching is the most valuable behavior toward the execution of the organization's strategy. Coaching is the *main thing* for that role. Therefore, individuals who demonstrate proficiency and effectiveness within the coaching practice are rewarded. What is the "main thing" for your current role? What is the most important activity for which you are accountable in your job description? Review and complete the exercise in figure 3.2 to discover your "main thing."

First, identify three of your most important job requirements. Then break down each requirement into the specific behaviors or actions you must take to meet it. For example, if a job requirement is to make a hotdog, then the corresponding behaviors would include cooking the hotdog, steaming the bun, and adding the condiments. This activity will help you focus on the specific actions you must take to achieve the critical functions of your role.

High-Value-Behavior Identification Exercise

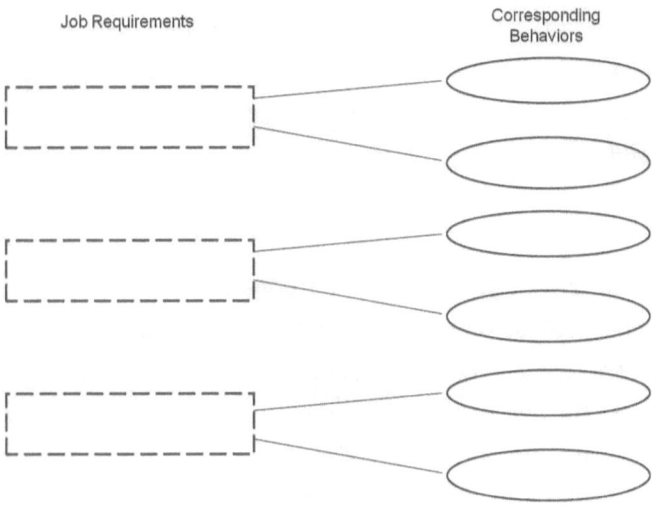

Job Requirements

Corresponding
Behaviors

Figure 3.2

When you get a new job, ask your supervisor, "What are the measures for success?" Know them and track your daily, weekly, and monthly performance against those measures.

The Annual Review

The annual review makes people nervous, and with good reason. This event is often the basis of raises and promotions, and it is tied to the job requirements of a role. Have you noticed a trend here? It is baffling how many professionals do not pay close attention to the basic requirements of their role.

This area is a huge point of differentiation for the top gen X and millennial professionals: Fast-track performers are keenly aware of their responsibilities and what success looks like for their roles. Do you know how you are evaluated during your annual review? What are the key metrics or categories that will drive your performance rating? These are critical questions that require quality responses if you plan to manage your career proactively and make it thrive.

If you can't answer these questions, I'd encourage you to set up a meeting with your boss tomorrow and get some answers. You may think you are performing at a high level, but your boss may not agree. You must understand how you are rated throughout the year so you can be intentional about performing in a way that aligns with the annual review rating you want. Your long-term career prospects are too important to drop the ball on this area.

Have you ever gone into an annual review conversation and been surprised by your rating? When we are surprised by an annual rating, it is often because we did not do a good job of tracking our performance against the requirements of our role throughout the year. That is an expensive mistake that can mean the difference between a 2 percent raise and a 10 percent raise. If you are anything like me, you want to get the maximum raise every time. Take a look at figure 3.3 to observe the difference in compensation of two employees over a five-year period, each with a starting salary of $50,000, when one gets the maximum raise each year and the other doesn't.

	Employee A 3% Annual Raise	Employee B 10% Annual Raise
Year 1	$50,000	$50,000
Year 2	$51,500	$55,000
Year 3	$53,045	$60,500
Year 4	$54,636.35	$66,550
Year 5	$56,275.44	$73,205

Figure 3.3

This is your career, not community service, right? If you are anything like my survey respondents, your compensation is one of the primary reasons you are in the workforce. It is difficult to argue with the adverse impact that a poor annual performance review has on your long-term career health and earning potential. The example above captured only a five-year span in the workforce. Imagine how being Employee A would impact you over the course of ten, twenty, or forty years in the workforce!

Of survey respondents, 35.2 percent don't understand the rating factors in their annual performance reviews.

Do What Your Company Asks

Okay, I get it. You looked at this section and thought, *Al is really stating the obvious here*. After all, we are hired by companies and organizations to perform specific tasks, trading our time for money, right? But hear me out. Take the next twenty seconds to write down the names of people in your office who sometimes "forget" to perform basic responsibilities within their job. Your list should include individuals who do a great job of *not* doing what your company asks of them. Grab a pen and start writing below.

_____   _____

_____   _____

_____   _____

How many names did you write down? One? Two? Ten? I'll bet you a steak dinner that a few names came to mind. Why is that? So many people go to work every day, omit basic responsibilities from their schedule, and exert energy to cover it up. In other words, many people go to work and don't do their jobs. Fast-track performers do what they are asked to do. This is such an easy way to differentiate yourself from your peers while adding value to your organization.

Your boss asks you to do things because your efforts will help with a responsibility for which he or she is accountable. Believe me, your boss knows who is doing what's required and who isn't. He or shew will remember when it is time to complete annual reviews and recommend employees for advancement opportunities. Doing the right thing allows you to become a part of the solution instead of being the face of the problem.

Someone holds your boss accountable for his or her results, so you do not want to be the cause of poor results. You should seize any opportunity to build genuine affinity with your boss. I am not a fan of the office "kiss-up." You can get ahead at work without kissing up to your boss so please do not misconstrue my comments. You have to determine where you stand on this issue. I firmly believe the fast-track performer does not need to worry about being a kiss-up. Fast-track performers only need to worry about how they can add differentiated value to their company.

Consistency, Consistency, Consistency

Robert Horry is regarded as one of the best clutch basketball players in NBA playoff history (Pauker 2011). His ability always to come up with the big play earned him the nickname "Big Shot Bob." Take a look at a few of the biggest shots of his career:

- 1995 NBA Finals, Game 3: Horry hit a three-pointer to give the Houston Rockets a 104–100 lead with 14.1 seconds remaining in the game. Houston won the NBA Championship.
- 2001 NBA Finals, Game 3: Horry hit a three-pointer to give the Los Angeles Lakers a 92–88 lead with 47.1 seconds remaining in the game. He then hit four free-throws to seal the victory. The Lakers won the NBA Championship.
- 2002 Western Conference Finals, Game 4: Horry hit a three-pointer as time expired to give the Los Angeles Lakers a

100–99 victory. The Lakers won that series and the NBA Championship.

Most of us are not 6'10" athletes with a great jump shot, but the good news is we don't need to make jump shots to do a great job at work. We can learn a lot from Robert Horry, who developed a reputation for consistently hitting big shots when it counted.

Consistency in performance is a major point of differentiation for the fast-track performer. It is easy to be a one-hit wonder, where you have a great month of sales production, nail a critical presentation, or get a project completed on time and under budget. But can you deliver high performance month after month, year after year? Your company needs professionals who bring their best game every day.

Most people in the workplace are inconsistent in their performance. Performance management systems align individual performance to organizational performance, so consistent performers tend to earn better reviews than inconsistent ones.

Robert Horry's consistency was rewarded with a long career and six championships. The average NBA career is 4.8 years (Coon 2011), but Horry played for seventeen seasons because every team he played for knew what it was getting when it added him to the payroll. What are you known for within your company? Does your boss view you as a valuable, known commodity? Consistent, high-value performance will get you there.

Find ways to ensure your performance is
consistent and reliable so your leadership team
will trust you with more responsibility.

Perspective from the Top

When employers are looking to hire for advancement, they look to the past to predict the future. Your past success will indicate future success. If you don't have a past you are proud of, chances are your future will be just as disappointing. To be respected by your future employees, past success is critical. That said, what I have learned in my career is that the person who is number one is not necessarily the best leader. The skill to teach someone how to be successful does not always lie with the person who has the best performance. In my career I always strived to the top in customer satisfaction but also balanced it with helping those around me succeed. My consistent performance was rewarded with increased opportunities and progressive promotions.

—S. H., vice president, higher education, generation X

Just Say No to Steroids

Have you ever worked with someone in your office who did such an exceptional job that it seemed that no one could ever fill his or her shoes? Everyone in the office probably believed that person was irreplaceable, and coworkers marveled at how the person knew so much about so many things. However, when the person was out of the office, his or her work came to a screeching halt because no one else could do what he or she did. It may seem like I am describing a fast-track performer, but this person *never* gets promoted.

If you are irreplaceable, you can't move to another role. If there is no one else who can add value to your position, you will remain stagnant because it is entirely too expensive for your organization to move you. What would you do if you were running a business and your employee was so good that he or she could effectively do the job of two people? Would you put him or her in a different role? Probably not. There is absolutely no incentive to promote such a person to greater responsibility because you would have to hire two people to replace him or her.

This kind of situation is unfortunate because irreplaceable professionals are usually talented and capable of doing more meaningful work. However, their inability to delegate important tasks and unwillingness to share their "secret sauce" are usually the drivers of their reality. People often believe it is important to take all the credit for strong performance, but fast-track performers seize opportunities to empower others. Their ability to help coworkers improve performance is a highly sought-after skill. Performance on steroids is not good in sports or the business world. Don't fall into that trap because you will certainly regret it.

Be Successful on Purpose

Every organization has people who do great work. I am sure you can identify people in your office whose performance you hold in high regard. Do you think they know exactly what they are doing to get solid results? The fast-track performer is keenly aware of the levers he or she pulls to maintain peak performance, but this is not a common skill set in the workplace. Ask most people in your office to share the specific behaviors that allow them to be successful, and you will probably get an incoherent response like "I don't know; I just do it" or "It is hard to explain."

It is important to be successful on purpose, as organizational leaders are inclined to look at the self-aware professional for advancement opportunities. This is another great point of differentiation and value, as this behavior will cause you to be viewed as competent and strategic as opposed to lucky. A good strategy can be replicated and scaled up, while luck can't.

Imagine your company is going through a major change initiative, and the management team is struggling to get results, but one manager's team is flourishing in the new structure. Everyone in the organization wants to know what actions this manager is taking to drive performance, but if the manager can't articulate his or her strategy, the organization can't capitalize on the team's success. If the manager was able to delineate a few high-impact behaviors that drove his or her success, their reputation and stature in the company would be strengthened. The manager would have differentiated himself or herself from everyone else and added a tremendous amount of value in the process.

Fast-track performers understand the importance of reflecting on their success regularly to identify best practices. Each time you have a career achievement, take some time to debrief by asking the following questions:

- At what point did my performance begin moving in a positive direction?
- What actions did I take during that time that changed my results?
- What behaviors, if replicated, are likely to get a similar result?
- Is there anything else I could have done to improve my performance?

These questions are important because they facilitate reflection and personal accountability and prepare you to articulate your strategy to anyone in your organization who asks. Your career will be served well if you always make time to reflect on your performance.

The Generational Application

Generation X

This strategy aligns perfectly with a key generation X trait: You have a laser focus on the task at hand, it is important to complete every task within your area of responsibility in a timely way, and you simply need to make sure you understand all of your role requirements so you can execute. You also like to be challenged. The tougher the job the better, right?

Your appreciation for smart structure underscores the importance of task execution, as structures work when all component parts operate effectively.

You value independence, and you are more likely to get the independence you crave when you do your job. There is nothing worse than an overbearing, micromanaging boss who does not trust your ability to get the job done, but you have to earn that flexibility. Your consistent performance will make it tough for any boss to find value in monitoring your every move.

Millennials

High performance is easy for you, so the challenge lies in your ability to be consistent. You are driven to succeed, and you typically desire to move onto the next role once you've demonstrated your ability to master your current role, but that perspective isn't practical. The business cycle and business need impact the job openings, so your company may not have a role for you to fill when you're ready for the next role. That reality may cause your performance to decline, but you have to fight that urge, remain focused on your current role, and maintain consistent performance. This may be particularly difficult if you are in an entry-level position that does not use all of your skills. It becomes even more difficult if you see people in your desired role with inferior skills. Just maintain a positive attitude and pay your dues in the entry-level role, which won't last long if you're a fast-track performer.

Recommended Reading

1. *Eat That Frog* by Brian Tracy
2. *The 7 Habits of Highly Effective People* by Stephen Covey
3. *First Things First* by Stephen Covey
4. *The Charge* by Brendon Burchard
5. *Getting Things Done: The Art of Stress-Free Productivity* by David Allen
6. *Patterns of High Performance: Discovering the Ways People Work Best* by Jerry Fletcher

Be
A
Professional

Advertise
Ambition

Study Your Craft

Be A Change Champion

Build Two-Way Relationships

Communicate Effectively

Perform Consistently

CHAPTER 4

COMMUNICATE EFFECTIVELY

"Communication works for those who work at it."
—John Powell, composer

More people are more afraid of speaking in public than they are of dying. Can you believe that? I am certain that presentations don't kill, but it is possible to create killer presentations that convey important messages effectively. The average person doesn't communicate well because he or she can't get past the fears associated with communicating to a group of people.

I have always wondered what it is about speaking in front of a team or leading a department meeting that makes people so nervous. Is it simply a fear of saying something stupid or incoherent? No matter the cause, effective communication is one of the most valuable behaviors exhibited by fast-track performers.

Consider some of the great communicators of our time: Dr. Martin Luther King, Ronald Reagan, Bill Clinton. Let's disregard their politics for a moment and evaluate their communication effectiveness. Did their ability to communicate add to or detract from their credibility? Effective communicators are admired because of their ability to connect with people and convey critical messages with apparent ease.

You don't have to be a famous orator to reap the benefits of savvy communication. Think about people you view as competent communicators—a former teacher, a colleague, or a pastor, for example. What is your overall impression of them? What effect do you think their communication ability has on your perception of them? Strong communicators are viewed as intelligent and capable. I asked my survey respondents to think of the attributes that they associate with the best communicators in their office. The most common responses to that question are listed in figure 4.1.

The Most Common Perceptions of Effective Communicators in the Workplace

Intelligent	Thoughtful
Great Listener	Fearless
Proactive	Clear
Visionary	Approachable
Optimistic	Strategic
Confident	Honest
Empathetic	Leader
Resourceful	

Figure 4.1

How valuable do you think you will be in the office if your coworkers' perception of you include a handful of those adjectives? There is no doubt you will easily stand out. Effective communicators have a high level of differentiation in the workplace, mainly because so many people struggle to master the skill. I know it sounds horrible but it is true. You don't have to take my word for it. Every day professionals have to sit through dry meetings and conference calls that make the most boring, monotone professors look like rock stars. How many uneventful meetings or presentations have you suffered through over the last thirty days? (I rest my case.) Strong written and verbal communication skills will help you increase your visibility and give you access to more opportunities.

Why Is It So Important?

Companies and organizations depend on strong communicators to explain priorities, change initiatives, and directives. In today's world of split-second tweets and Facebook posts, a strong communication structure is essential, as the gears of a company can't turn without clarity of task.

Think of the last major change that occurred in your workplace. How well was it communicated? Did you have questions about the actions you needed to take? Lack of clarity paralyzes productivity, and you certainly don't want to be the cause of a colleague's confusion. What if you were regarded as a resource with an uncanny ability to convey even the most complex message? You would be highly valued, and that is never a bad thing.

Many—even most—people struggle with clear and concise communication. I am reminded of an exercise I participated in during a communication workshop. The facilitator was a savvy professional named Johnny who reminded me of my grandfather. In the middle of the workshop, he lined everyone up and said he wanted us to transfer a message from one end of the line to the other, a game of telephone. At that moment I knew exactly what he expected to happen. Johnny thought we were going to fumble the message, but I knew that wouldn't happen because I was in a room of fifteen adults. I'd be skeptical if fifteen giggling teenagers were tasked to do this, but I knew we would prove Johnny wrong.

He went to the other end of the line and whispered into a participant's ear, and the message began moving down the line. When it was my turn, I closed my eyes in hopes of heightening my hearing sense and then transferred the message flawlessly. The message made it to the end of the line and Johnny was right there waiting for it. When the last participant relayed the message, Johnny began to laugh. Clearly, we fifteen adults had fallen victim to this exercise, as the original message, "I take life as it comes . . . come what will," became "My life is almost done . . . write my will." Strategic messages are fumbled during staff meetings and impromptu conversations near the coffee machine every day.

Strong communicators are a necessity for executing business strategy, which makes them highly valued resources.

The best companies have the most effective and robust communication mechanisms: company intranet websites, newsletters, periodic leadership communications, internal social media platforms, and others. These tools are all great, but they must be supported by an old-school tool: the conversation. Leaders have to master the basic conversation, where the goal is to transmit a message in a way that facilitates understanding and buy-in.

Companies must know that their leaders can ensure that messages are transferred in a way that allows the receiving employees to act on them. Have you ever had a boss tell you to do something, and after you began working he or she came back and said that what you were doing was not what he or she wanted? How frustrating is that? Great communicators rarely have that issue. The work of an organization can't get done properly without a team of effective communicators. Therein lies the value of effective communication. Fast-track performers are effective communicators, and they bring significant value to the table.

The ability to communicate effectively has always been an important skill in the workplace, but it is even more valuable in the twenty-first century workforce. The proliferation of the participative leadership style along with efforts to bolster employee empowerment create the demand for strong communicators. Senior executives commonly solicit feedback from entry-level employees and front-line leaders to improve performance. Organizations leverage employee perspectives via surveys, focus groups, and town hall meetings. This new workforce needs professionals who can communicate effectively up, down, and across. In the communication structure image in figure 4.2, you will notice that communication occurs between managers and their direct reports, senior executives, and front-line leaders, and from the chief-level officers all the way down to entry-level employees. Each one of these conversations requires a different approach because the audiences are different. Professionals at all levels must demonstrate the ability to communicate in all of these settings in order to add value to their organization.

Communication Structure

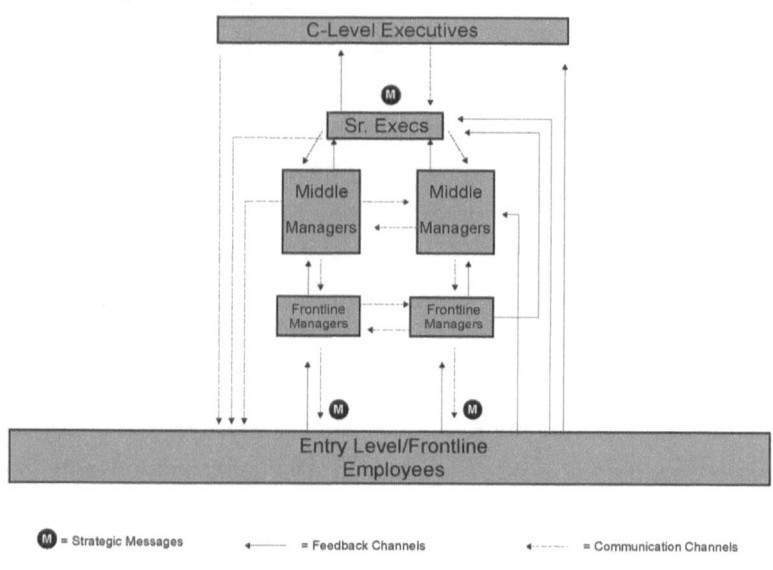

Figure 4.2

Perspective from the Top

I use my communication skills daily. I am the liaison between the people in the field who talk to clients and generate business and the people in the office who underwrite and approve the deals. Since I often facilitate the underwriting discussion, I must communicate the strengths and weaknesses of a potential deal effectively. I often have to work with my team in the field and determine the creditworthiness of a commercial client. I always try to be clear, open, and honest, and I like to back up all of my ideas with facts so

I can articulate my positions better. It is one thing to say a business is strong; it is another to say a business is strong because they have x amount of dollars in cash, low debt, and a strong customer base. If I can't back up my ideas with facts, then I don't have anything valuable to offer. I am in charge of 250 credit clients totaling $3.6 billion in assets, so I have a number of these interactions every day. My ability to communicate with clarity allows me to be effective in my role. I like to call a spade a spade, and I am not afraid to piss people off when I know I am doing the right thing.

—S. E., vice president, financial services industry, generation X

Sixty-seven percent of all survey respondents are required to make presentations to execute their job requirements.

Everything Is for Sale

I am a sales guy. Most of my career has been spent selling a product or supporting a sales organization. Everyone walking this beautiful earth has an innate ability and desire to sell. You may not agree if you view salespeople as sleazy, conniving people whose only goal is the suck their customers' pockets dry. However, I will take it a step further and suggest nothing happens in the world until a sale is made. Consider the following sales events:

1. Parents sell their children on the idea of cleaning their room, eating vegetables, and brushing their teeth.
2. Teachers sell students on the idea of studying and doing homework.

3. Every four years American citizens are inundated by sophisticated sales campaigns for the presidency of the United States.
4. A wife gets her husband to stop watching *SportsCenter* so she can watch *The Real Housewives of Atlanta.*
5. Someone sold my publisher the paper that created the pages of this book and the ink that was used to print the words on each page.

You may wonder what this all has to do with the ability to communicate effectively. Think about the last time a boss got you to do something with which you did not initially agree. Your boss probably engaged in an effective conversation and discussed what needed to be done, why it was important, and why you needed to comply with the request. He or she even answered some of your questions to ensure you understood how to proceed. After a little bit of back-and-forth conversation, your boss reiterated the request and got your commitment to comply. Bottom line, your boss sold you on doing what he or she wanted. Great communicators are smart salespeople who find ways to get others to buy in to their ideas and recommendations. This behavior expands the reach of influence and increases their value to organizations.

I don't want to focus too much on selling. However, it is imperative that you understand that you "sell" ideas, actions, and plans every day. If you don't like the salesperson label, we can call you an influencer.

Let's apply this influencer idea to your life. Take five minutes to complete the activity in figure 4.3. For each column, think about a time when you initially disagreed with a person but ultimately aligned with his or her idea. Describe the specific situation, your concerns that caused the disagreement, and how you ultimately adopted his or her perspective. For example, under the "spouse" column I would write about a disagreement with my wife about the need for a videographer at our wedding. I was concerned about the additional expense because I thought a photographer would do a good job and capture all of our special memories. I quickly realized that the bride tends to get everything she wants when it comes to her wedding, so I embraced the videographer idea and the additional expense.

	Coworker	Spouse	Parent
Situation			
Your Concerns			
Describe how you aligned with their perspective			

Figure 4.3

There is typically a six-step process to influence someone to your point of view, which is identical to the general sales/influencing process. Selling and influencing are both an art and a science.

Of survey respondents who have been promoted in the last five years, 88.8 percent believe sales ability is a valuable career advancement behavior.

Step 1—Identify your "customer."

This "customer" is the person you want to persuade to adopt your idea or proposal. This person can be your superior, a peer, or a direct report.

Step 2—Determine his or her need.

Identify all the reasons that can motivate your customer to support your idea. What must happen before you can gain his or her support? Maybe your customer's last project failed and he or she wants to redeem himself or herself. Maybe he or she is close to a promotion, and a strong showing on a new project can secure the new role. Maybe he doesn't want a videographer at his wedding. When you understand a person's motivations, you can frame your request in a way that appeals to those motives.

Step 3—Highlight the features and benefits of your idea.

The features are the basic components of your idea, the specific parameters and logistics. An effective feature presentation must connect with your customer's logical side.

Example of features presentation: I want to start a new mentoring program that will target all of the first-year managers. The mentors will meet with their mentees once per month to discuss best practices in the area of leadership.

The benefits describe what the features will do for the audience; they are the solution to a problem. This portion of the idea presentation must connect with the audience's emotional side. People tend to buy in to ideas based on emotion and justify the buy-in with logic.

Example of benefits presentation: This mentoring program will increase the performance of our first-year managers in every major performance metric by 10 percent. You are looking for a way to demonstrate your project management skills, and the mentoring program is a great opportunity to show those skills. This is a win-win proposition for both you and our first-year managers.

Step 4—Ask for commitment.

The most important part of any idea presentation is to ask for agreement. After you make your request, you must have a commitment from your customer that he or she will move forward and support the idea. Many people spend too much time explaining their idea and fail to move beyond the explanation stage and ask for the other party's support. You can ask for their support in a number of ways:

- "How does that sound to you?"
- "Can I count on your support during the staff meeting?"
- "Are you ready to make this happen?"
- "Does this sound like an idea you can support?"

As you can see, all of these questions put the ball back in your customer's court, and he or she must respond by accepting your idea, asking clarifying questions, delaying an answer, or rejecting the proposal outright.

Step 5—Answer questions and address resistance.

Most people will have questions about your proposal and will need satisfactory answers to each question before they can make a decision. Respond to each question thoroughly and ask whether your answer gave your customer the required clarity. If your customer offers resistance, ask questions so you can understand the source of the apprehension. Once you uncover the source, make adjustments to your proposal where you can in order to make your customer comfortable in offering support.

Step 6—Ask for commitment . . . again.

After clearing up the remaining questions and resistance, it is time to ask for your customer's support again in order to solidify your agreement.

This is a basic explanation of the persuasive process. Again, individuals who can influence others stand out because of their high level of differentiation in the workplace.

Perspective from the Top

My job and my field are all about persuasion. In my previous role I worked for a national nonprofit organization that often held blood drives. The blood from the drives was a major source of revenue that funded other parts of the organization. I needed to persuade my donor recruitment department to reach out to underrepresented minority populations to increase the number of donors. I noticed there was a large gap between our typical donor population and the need for people of color to get blood transfusions, but I had to convince my CEO and the recruitment department leadership to invest in my plan to launch a new advertising campaign and allocate more dedicated recruiters to minority communities. They were hesitant about moving forward with my plan because it required a considerable investment, so I had to research the problem thoroughly and present my plan as the best solution. I was able to quantify the need for and the deficit of minority blood donors in my four-state region. I also took the time to outline the harsh reality that there are people who need blood but can't get it because organizations like mine have not made the issue a priority. In addition, I forecasted the amount of revenue this initiative could generate for the organization, estimating that this program would bring in $1 million in revenue. That is a significant sum of money for a nonprofit organization. Ultimately, everyone decided to move forward with my plan. I had to know my audience and understand what made them tick, as this knowledge helped me put my proposal in a language they understood and appreciated. My proposal was a great initiative because it now generates over $2 million in revenue and serves 1,300 patients, and the program has yet to reach its full potential. The biggest lesson I learned from this experience is that the important thing about great ideas is that they must get implemented. People often try to present their ideas in a manner that guarantees they get the credit, but this initiative taught me that I need to present my ideas in a way that makes it easy for others to say it was their idea. That approach is tough for new professionals because everyone is so busy looking for the next feather to add to their caps. This can shock your pride but it increases your influence.

—E. D., senior manager, defense industry, millennial

Once upon a Time

My fiancée and I love to catch a good movie. There is something magical about how a great story can transport us to another place without our ever leaving our seats.

In 2011, American theaters sold roughly 1.29 billion movie tickets. The gross revenue from those ticket sales was $10.28 billion (The Numbers 2012). Over the 2011–2012 season, Broadway recorded $1.13 billion in revenue (Statistica 2012). Americans—in fact, all human beings in all cultures—love stories.

I hear stories while at the barbershop, during Sunday church sermons, and on Monday morning at the office. We have all listened to coworkers talk about their weekend highlights. If we have to communicate dull organizational strategies and project work plan updates, doesn't it make sense to attach a story whenever possible?

It is easier to remember a story that illustrates a concept than a concept without a story. Stories have a rhythm, and they take you on a journey. The brain struggles to remember boring things, so it is incumbent upon you as a communicator to liven them up (Medina 2008).

Let's be honest: we work with a lot of boring data at work. Do your coworkers a favor and spice up your communication a bit. The good news is the retention of the communicated information will increase, and retained information is more likely to become actionable information. The fast-track performer understands this and is able to deliver messages that stick.

Herb Kelleher, one of the founders of Southwest Airlines, used to tell a simple story as he traveled around the country making site visits. It was a powerful story that identified Southwest's competitors and explained its business strategy in less than two minutes. Kelleher often said, "It's funny; I get letters all the time from shareholders, and they're often angry letters. They say, 'America West is flying from Los Angeles to Vegas for $149 one way and you are pricing that same one-way ticket at $79. Don't you at least have the decency to kick your price up to $129? Why are you leaving so much on the table?'"

Kelleher would go on to say, "What I do is write back and reply, 'Thank you for your letter. However, you don't really understand who we are and you really don't understand who our competition is. It's the automobile—it's not the airlines—and $79 is the price to drive, including maintenance, insurance, and gasoline, from Los Angeles to Las Vegas. That's how we price our tickets.'"

Kelleher would use that simple story to drive home the entire organizational strategy to every employee down to the baggage handler. That is a great story, isn't it? A story is far more powerful than a twenty-slide PowerPoint presentation, and it is easier to recall than any other corporate communication vehicle. Simplicity is the key.

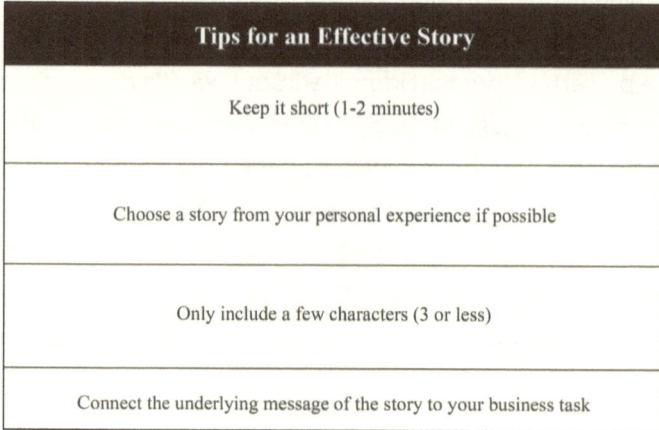

Figure 4.4

Perspective from the Top

I have always believed if a kindergartener doesn't understand what you are saying, your message may get lost. Leaders often want to give high-level overviews of simple concepts, but highbrow language is not necessary all the time. We should communicate on the simplest level so anyone can understand us. I believe people should see and feel your comments. It is kind of like changing a tire: I can give you a wordy presentation about how to change a tire that's full of charts and graphs, or I can use a story or anecdote to help you understand the process. At the end of the day, you want people to act upon your ideas so you can get results. I like to paint pictures in their simplest form so my team can execute with ease.

—A. W. B., territory manager, automotive industry, generation X

Components of a Story

Figure 4.5

Tap and Transport

I have talked quite a bit about the use of stories as a communication tool, so you may be wondering about the best way to incorporate stories into your presentations. You can't call a meeting and read Dr. Seuss books to your colleagues, but there is a subtle and effective way to add stories to your toolkit.

About four years ago I met Craig Valentine, the 1999 World Champion of Public Speaking. Toastmasters International has been a big part of my life, and he was the keynote speaker at the North Carolina state competition. Craig encouraged me to use questions to set up my stories. The idea is to tap into your audience's world with a question, and then transport them into your world with a story related to that question (Myerson et al. 2009). This approach is effective because the question meets the audience where they are and triggers their mental participation in your presentation. It's a simple way to engage your audience, regardless of the topic.

Stories are a great way to communicate. Try to incorporate a quick story in your next meeting to bolster your points. Your colleagues will notice a difference, and they will appreciate your efforts to liven up your presentation. If you can develop a reputation in your office such that everyone looked forward to your meetings and comments, you'd carve out a major area of differentiation against your peers.

The Generational Application

Generation X

You enjoy direct communication. This is a valuable trait because you understand the importance of clear and concise communication. Your only challenge is to diversify your communication style. Direct communication is best for certain audiences, but make sure you know your audience so you can determine the most appropriate communication style.

You also like a laid-back and uncomplicated work environment, so incorporate stories into your communication to add a layer of informality to your work. The stories will also help improve the effectiveness of your communication.

You appreciate behaviors that allow you to get things done efficiently. Your ability to communicate your thoughts has a direct impact on your ability to get things done and be successful. It is particularly important for you to hone your ability to influence those around you, so pay close attention to your proficiency in this area.

Millennials

You love email and voicemail, but make sure you know when you have to have a face-to-face conversation. Sometimes it is more appropriate to walk down the hall to a colleague's office to continue a conversation than it is to keep sending emails. Many boomers prefer that face-to-face interaction.

You enjoy technology, so make sure your PowerPoint presentations are easy to follow. Your ability to incorporate stories into your communication will help you add the layer of informality to the workplace that you need and many of your colleagues will appreciate.

These Resources Can Help Right Now

1. Join a Toastmasters club in your office or community. This is a great way to improve your verbal communication skills. An annual membership is less than $150. Go to www.toastmasters.org.
2. Visit www.craigvalentine.com and subscribe to his newsletter, which is full of practical, easy-to-implement tips to improve your communication skills.
3. *Whoever Tells the Best Story Wins* by Annette Simmons

4. *Messages: The Communication Skills Book* by Matthew McKay, Martha Davis, and Patrick Fanning
5. *World Class Speaking* by Craig Valentine and Mitch Meyerson
6. *Presentation Secrets of Steve Jobs* by Carmine Gallo
7. *Presentation Zen* by Gar Reynolds
8. *How to Overcome Public Speaking Fear* by Arlen Busenitz
9. *Secrets of Closing the Sale* by Zig Ziglar
10. *Pitch Anything* by Oren Klaff
11. *The Science of Influence* by Kevin Hogan

Be
A
Professional

Advertise
Ambition

Study Your Craft

Be A Change Champion

Build Two-Way Relationships

Communicate Effectively

Perform Consistently

CHAPTER 5

BUILD TWO-WAY RELATIONSHIPS

"You can have everything in life you want if you will
just help enough people get what they want."
—Zig Ziglar, speaker and sales expert

I have a confession to make. I used to belong to a secret club of good men whose significant others lured us into the world of the Kardashians. You may want to revoke my man card and sentence me to a life of daytime soap operas and bubble baths, but first let me share a principle I witnessed on a recent episode of *Lamar and Khloe.*

Khloe's family had flown to Dallas to attend a Mavericks game and watch Lamar play. Kris, Khloe's mom, knew everyone, including Mavericks owner Mark Cuban. She reached out to him prior to her trip. Cuban put her in a penthouse suite and reserved his box for the family at the game. Kris Jenner knows people and always finds a way to make her connections work.

Malcom Gladwell described this phenomenon more eloquently in his book *The Tipping Point* (2002). He'd suggest Kris Jenner is a connector, someone who brings together people, ideas, and resources. We all have that one friend or relative who seems to have met every person on the planet. Every time you go out with him or her, this friend seems to run into someone they know. If you told this friend that your brakes were squeaking, he or she would come to the rescue like Tony Soprano, saying, "I've got a guy. Go see him and tell him I sent you."

These kinds of people always know what's going on, and they have a network of contacts for which any New York auction house could fetch a handsome sum of money. You certainly value that relationship. Most people find their relationships with connectors to be valuable, and if connectors are valued in personal and social settings, how do you think they are regarded in the workplace?

Everyone Is in the People Business

I began my college career at Bradley University as an electrical engineering major. It seemed to be the most appropriate major since math and science were my favorite subjects in high school, and the potential entry-level pay didn't hurt either. No disrespect to my engineering brothers and sisters, but I don't think my personality aligned with that of the typical engineer.

I entered college on the heels of a hyperactive community-organizing stint that took me to the White House for a taping of *Good Morning America*. That experience required me to work with people to get results—something I was good at. The engineering field was not a people-intense profession.

I will never forget my electrical circuits class. It was taught by a professor who would have made Ben Stein seem like Flava Flav. His class was the perfect place for me to catch up on sleep. After a week of his lectures, I'd had enough.

One introspective academic-advising session later, I decided to change my major to speech communications. I was a self-proclaimed "people person" and was convinced I would not get to work with people if I became an engineer.

Conventional wisdom suggests some careers require people skills, while others don't, but that is a load of crap. We are all in the people business, no matter what career we choose. Engineers and accountants need to work with their colleagues to get things done just as much as the salesperson or public relations consultant does.

There is an ongoing competition for people, ideas, and resources throughout every organization in America. Malcolm Gladwell described the connector as someone who brings all of these things together. Connectors make things happen in the workplace, and the fast-track performer falls into this category.

Perspective from the Top

I typically try to get to know colleagues as people, that is, their interests, passions, and what they do outside of work. The deeper you get to know someone, the better chance you have at an effective working relationship. Too many people have the impression that you can't get personal with your coworkers because it may cross the business boundaries. You don't have to be professional all the time. If the relationship is too impersonal, you may not be willing to listen to them fully and give them the benefit of the doubt during interactions. It also allows you to be more open with each other. I make it a point to get to know my staff in the office but also vendors I work with. I am a CPA, and I have a better chance at getting referrals if someone knows more about me than just my work. When I get a referral, people talk about the quality of my work, but they also talk about who I am as a person.

—J. D., accountant, business owner, millennial

The Team Era

Gone are the days when tasks were completed by a lone worker; everything today is done in a team. The proliferation of work teams was a response to the globalization of the US economy and the early adoption of the team structure by highly visible organizations like General Motors, AT&T, General Electric, Xerox, and Motorola (Cristina et al. 1998). Teams became a necessity because there were fewer managers to keep track of employees' daily activities. In addition, work teams developed a track record of increased productivity, customer satisfaction, and job satisfaction. The twenty-first-century workforce has a strong connection to the team structure. Task forces, project teams, working groups, and committees are more productive when the team members develop sound relationships. Relationships matter.

When Terrell Owens was traded to the Philadelphia Eagles in 2004, everyone thought a Super Bowl victory was imminent. The Eagles had a talented quarterback in Donovan McNabb, a playmaking wide receiver with Terrell Owens, and a great defense. Conventional wisdom suggested Owens was the missing link. McNabb and Owens did not have the best working relationship. Their soap opera caused dissention within the team and a squandered opportunity to win a championship. Apparently the feud started during week 12 of the 2004 season. Owens thought he was open for a touchdown, but McNabb didn't throw him the ball (Smith 2006). That incident ignited a fiery feud that still causes Eagles fans nightmares. If McNabb and Owens's relationship had been better, the team's performance would have been better. We all know how this story ended. The Eagles lost to the Patriots in the Super Bowl, Donovan McNabb remained the starting quarterback, and Terrell Owens was deactivated before the end of the 2005 season.

Although you don' plan to lace up your cleats and step onto the gridiron, you can still learn something from this story. Don't be the Terrell Owens of your work team because you just might find yourself out of a job.

Liked or Respected?

Whether you prefer to be liked or respected is a classic leadership question that people discuss in MBA classrooms all across the world. It's a misplaced question, though, because it implies that the two traits are mutually exclusive. I have worked with people who were liked but not respected, respected but not liked, and well liked and well respected.

Of course, most people prefer to work with people whom they both like and respect. While work is not a popularity contest—a professional's primary objective is to perform his or her required tasks—everyone is in the people business. Work is more enjoyable when you can work with individuals you like.

Think of someone in your office whom you do not particularly like. Do you enjoy working with that person? Probably not. Organizational leaders have to consider the "people issues" associated with promoting one person over another. Whom do you think your boss would promote if he or she had two people who were qualified to fill a new role, but one was well liked and the other was not? It's not a difficult question. Your boss may see adverse result If they promote the qualified person whom no one likes. There is likely to be a drop in employee morale, engagement, and motivation that crushes productivity. You don't want to be the person at the helm when that bad decision gets implemented. The bottom line is that your relationships matter. The quality of your relationships affects whether people like working with you.

Of survey respondents, 84.1 percent believe building relationships is a strong career-advancement behavior.

The Two-Way Relationship

There are many horror stories regarding relationship building in the workplace. You have heard of the person who smiles in your face but will to stab you in the back to get ahead. What about the person who kisses up to every bigwig in the company? These office caricatures are not professionals; they are opportunists who manufacture one-sided interactions and are too lazy to build real relationships.

Fast-track performers invest their time in building relationships that are based upon mutual benefits, where both people believe they get something from the relationship. These relationships take work, but they are valuable. In one-sided relationships, one person is always on the losing end of interactions. No one wants to lose all the time. The opportunist always takes from his or her relationships and rarely gives anything. It's like making frequent withdrawals from a "relationship bank account" without making any deposits. Eventually you will run out of relationships. One-sided relationships are short-lived because the other person gets tired of being used.

Now consider a two-way relationship, where you look for ways to give to and add value to the other person. Your giving builds up a pretty handsome "relationship bank account" of goodwill that allows you to make a withdrawal when you need one.

Bob Burg and John David Mann, authors of *The Go-Giver* (2007), crystallize the inherent value of giving to others in the context of business relationships. They mention three laws that can be used as a framework for building effective workplace relationships: *The law of value* states that your true worth is determined by how much more you give in value than you take in payment. How would you characterize the health of your workplace relationships? Do you give more than you take? This is an important question because it represents the foundation of your ability to build sustainable win-win relationships.

The law of influence says that your influence is determined by how often you place other people's interests first, as it is difficult to dislike someone who understands and cares about your needs. How often are your intentions and goals misunderstood in the workplace? How well do you understand others' intentions and goals? How often do you put them ahead of your own?

Finally, *the law of authenticity* states that the most valuable gift you have to offer is your true self. You can't maximize the relationship-building potential of this strategy if you don't have a genuine interest in helping others be successful. The implementation of this giving strategy may require you accept a complete paradigm shift, from focusing more on yourself to focusing more on others, but try the approach and judge the results for yourself.

This approach to giving of ourselves taps into our innate desire to repay favors in kind. When you give something of value, the receiving party feels compelled to give you something of value in return. Maybe you have a friend who is always there for you and willing to lend a hand. That friend probably does not ask you for much at all, but if he or she ever did ask you for a favor, even a big favor, it would be difficult to say no.

Nonprofit organizations have already discovered the value of this approach. When fundraisers enclose a small gift in an envelope to potential donors, the volume of donations significantly increases. This is human nature at its best. I recently received a nice set of return-address labels in the mail from a charity that I have worked with in the past. The address labels are very nice, and I am looking forward to using them. What else do you think the charity included in the envelope? Yes, a self-addressed, postage-paid envelope for my financial donation. This is an effective strategy because I almost feel that my mother would be disappointed in me if I didn't reciprocate. Have you ever found yourself in a similar situation?

You may think this strategy sounds manipulative, and I'll admit it can be leveraged with ill intent. However, I believe you always get more of what you want when you are willing to give first. Fast-track performers get tremendous satisfaction from helping others in the workplace, and people love working with them. That goodwill, coupled with strong performance, makes them ideal candidates for promotion opportunities.

The two-way relationship offers a significant amount of differentiation from others in your office because most people build one-sided relationships. I encourage you to focus on being a reliable resource for others over the next thirty days and observe how people respond to you.

Perspective from the Top

A foundation of authenticity and trust is important to building a relationship. I think it is important to be willing to serve as a resource to others. You have to put yourself out there and also be willing to demonstrate the things you stand for. Gen X and millennials have a bad reputation for being takers. I have not had that experience. It is important to understand that just because you have a certain job now does not mean you will be in the same place next year or the year after, so you should network inside and outside of your company. People who are resources can always go out to folks they have helped and ask for a favor. More often than not, they are more than willing to become a resource for you. People who have never been a resource for someone don't know where to go when they are in a pinch. When you become a resource, you are simultaneously building a network of resources that you can tap in the future.

—J. P., executive director, nonprofit, generation X

Seek First to Understand

In Dale Carnegie's epic book, *How to Win Friends and Influence People* (1936), Carnegie suggests you should seek first to understand, then to be understood. This is a powerful relationship-building strategy because it is firmly focused on the other person. Too often, we want to make sure the other person understands our point of view before we are willing to explore why the person holds his or her perspective. If you take a step back from any argument or disagreement, it will become apparent that everyone involved is interested in being heard, understood, and respected. It is that desire for our ideas to be taken seriously that becomes the source of conflict and miscommunication.

What would happen if you pursued an approach that gives others an opportunity to share their perspective and be heard? Do you think that they will then be more willing to give your ideas the time, attention, and respect they deserve? I do.

When I was growing up, I noticed that many of my parents' arguments began when one of them felt as though his or her ideas were not listened to or properly respected. I can just hear my mother saying, "William, since you aren't listening to me and won't let me talk, I will just be quiet." Now that I have some of my own experience with relationships, I wonder how many arguments could have been avoided if my parents had always been willing to try to understand the other's position *before* they shared their perspective.

There is one thing you can do right now to integrate this tactic into your behavior at work: take an interest in other people's work. Reach out to coworkers in and out of your department, focusing your interest on

- the projects they are currently working on,
- the projects they would like to work on,
- current challenges on their plate, and
- recent successes they have experienced.

There are so many other benefits to this strategy. First, you enhance your perspective of your company's work. A broad perspective of your company's strategy helps you connect the dots and align your work with organizational strategy. Second, you will build a reputation as a competent and curious professional. Every professional needs to have strong learning agility in order to adapt to change quickly and acquire new skills. Third, and the biggest point of differentiation, is that most people have this type of conversation only with their direct managers.

It feels good to be able to share your perspective about work challenges and successes with colleagues. Many people feel overworked and undervalued, and they don't always get the opportunity to market their work to anyone but their bosses. Fast-track performers give their coworkers an additional outlet to talk openly about their work.

Perspective from the Top

I built my professional reputation on my ability to fix underperforming car dealerships. I would be assigned to the worst auto dealership in my organization, with the expectation that I'd engineer its return to profitability. In 1998 I was assigned to a particularly troubling dealership with many problems. Within ninety days I took the business from losing more than $300,000 each month to the break-even point. After another ninety days, we were able to generate a profit. During the turnaround, I eliminated and saved a number of jobs, and one of the men whose job I saved eventually became my boss. He had some resentment toward me because I saved the dealership, and he wanted that credit. I also coached and developed him to improve his overall performance. He called me into his office for a chat after my efforts led the us to become the top dealership in the country. During the conversation he raised my department's sales quota by more than 300 percent and told me that if I did not get the team to hit the quota, he would fire me. I couldn't believe he was serious. After that meeting I went to every single employee in my department and informed them of the conversation I had with my boss. I had one-on-one conversations with every team member, from the mechanics to the receptionists, the detailers, and the human resources staff and told them I *personally* needed their help. Everyone bought into the challenge, and we didn't just hit the quota, we crushed it! The most important lesson I learned was that you can ask a coworker for almost anything when you've established a strong relationship. The time it takes to build a strong relationship is an investment that will eventually pay off.

—A. W. B., territory manager, automotive industry, generation X

Clique Access or Membership?

High school was a great chapter in my life. Like most people I found a way to navigate those interesting adolescent years. One of my most vivid memories of high school is the wide variety of cliques. We had the basketball players, the cheerleaders, the student government crowd, and of course, the nerds. Cliques were always together; they went to class together, ate lunch together, and found each other in the hallways between classes.

Although many things from high school remain in the past where they should be, cliques seem to have staying power. We have cliques in the workplace. The workplace cliques eat lunch together, sit next to each other during meetings, and socialize with each other during breaks and happy hours. These groups are concentrations of power in the office. So what's the problem?

Perils of Membership

If you belong to a clique, someone in another group may discount what you do and say because you belong to that group. Cliques are just as powerful in the office as they were in homeroom classes. They affect the relationship-building process.

Your range of influence can decrease when you join a clique, as other groups may have difficulty seeing past your clique membership even when you bring forward sound proposals. Does it make sense to mute your influence by preferring one group of people over another? The ability to influence others is a foundational skill that fast-track performers use to grow their careers.

Benefits of Access

Although membership in cliques carries disadvantages, you cannot just ignore them, as clique members are still your colleagues. We should not act as if they are horrible people. You may want to consider gaining access to cliques without becoming a member.

One nasty by-product of a clique is groupthink, which occurs when the relationships in the group become so important that differences of opinion among members become all but taboo. This is dangerous in the workplace because it can affect the quality of work. You will have access to these groups if you are willing to acknowledge areas where you agree and to disagree without being disagreeable. The fact that you are willing to disagree with such an insulated group may disqualify you from membership, but your willingness to be respectful and listen to their ideas may gain you some credibility.

Of survey respondents, 45 percent have casual conversations with coworkers prior to starting their workdays.

Relationship Check-Up

Writing your ideas or concepts down on paper often brings clarity, and a similar process can help you think critically about the current state of your work relationships.

Make a list of everyone in your office who can help you execute your responsibilities. Consider administrative staff, organizational leaders, your boss, and workers in other departments. Write their names below.

_____   _____

_____   _____

_____   _____

Now list everyone in your office who can adversely affect your ability to execute your responsibilities. Consider individuals who may be opposed to some of the projects and responsibilities of your role, perhaps because they do not agree with your strategy. Think also about individuals who are in a role with veto power or who can restrict the parameters of your work. Write their names below.

_____   _____

_____   _____

_____   _____

Now it is time to transfer the names to figure 5.1. The idea is to plot all of the names you listed in several concentric circles, with you in the center. List the people who have the biggest impact on your role closest to you, in the inner circles, and the people with minimal impact on your role farther away from you, in the outer circles. Once you get all the names into the circles, take a step back and take it all in.

You have just identified everyone in your office with whom you must build solid two-way relationships. Your ability to do your job effectively is connected to your ability to get all of the colleagues on your list on your side. Either you have to align with their point of view, or you must get them to buy in to your perspective. This activity will help you be far more strategic about whom you build relationships with and why those relationships are so important.

I encourage you to revisit this list regularly, perhaps at the beginning of each year or after an organizational change. It should be a dynamic document to which you make changes when necessary.

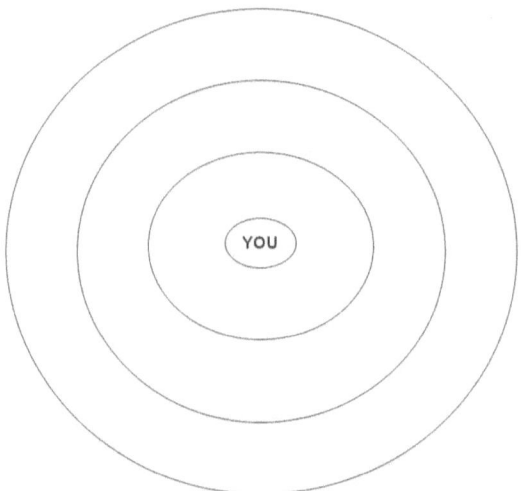

Figure 5.1

The Generational Application

Generation X

You are the middle generation of the workforce, and you need to build relationships with both boomers and millennials. The boomers are critical for you because you are their most likely replacement. Who can you solicit as a mentor to soak up valuable knowledge? Find ways to add value to their work. The millennials are an attractive group to connect with because of their ability to innovate and change things for the better. Harness their strengths via real relationships.

You don't mind working in teams, but you approach teamwork in a way that highlights the individual strengths of the team. Your ability to identify and leverage every team member's strengths is a skill that can add value to your organization, but be careful not to appear to dislike the idea of teamwork, as that could adversely impact your workplace relationships. Poor work relationships only make it more difficult for you to be successful at your work.

Millennials

You have spent a large part of your life as a member of teams, clubs, and organizations, so the rise of teams in the workplace is right in your relationship wheelhouse. Your ability to be a valuable contributor to your workplace team is critical to your career success. Spend time building relationships with everyone in your office—even the boomers and generation X colleagues, who may be close to your parents' age, as they can help you navigate the political terrain of your office. Don't make the mistake of restricting your relationships to fellow millennials, and remember the pending knowledge gap as a result of the boomer retirements. Develop a strategy to help you soak up as much of that knowledge as possible.

You are a talented person, so be willing to share your knowledge. Keep in mind that the boomers and gen X believe your generation is pretty arrogant, so don't be a know-it-all when you share your knowledge. That will backfire on you and make it more difficult to build relationships with people in your office.

These Resources Can Help Right Now

1. Join a civic organization. Increase your community involvement, and build relationships outside of the workplace. Identify a couple of causes that are important to you, and look for organizations in your community that promote them.
2. *The Tipping Point* by Malcolm Gladwell
3. *Linchpin* by Seth Godin
4. *Drive* by Daniel Pink
5. *The Go-Giver* by Bob Burg
6. *Problematic Relationships in the Workplace* by Janie Harden Fritz and Becky Omdahl
7. *The Speed of Trust* by Stephen M. R. Covey
8. *How to Win Friends and Influence People* by Dale Carnegie
9. *Secrets to Winning at Office Politics* by Marie McIntyre
10. *The Hard Truth about Soft Skills* by Peggy Klaus

CHAPTER 6

BE A CHANGE CHAMPION

"Change is inevitable, except from a vending machine."
—Robert C. Gallagher, business leader

My mother is a self-described coffee addict. Seriously, if there was ever a Coffee Anonymous group, she would be the founding member. She proudly proclaims caffeine is her drug of choice. I guess there are worse drugs out there, so she isn't doing too bad. My siblings and I understand our mother's addiction. You could even consider us her chief enablers. When I was a child, this scene occurred every Saturday morning in my house:

"Tony! Mikey! Chris! Al!" she would yell. Whenever Mom called us, we knew she expected us to come to wherever she was in the house. We affectionately call her the brigadier general of the family.

A flurry of footsteps would scurry to her room, and when we were all lined up, we'd say, "Yes, ma'am."

"I need you all to go get me some coffee from McDonald's. I have a little headache. You know what I want, right?"

My brother Chris always jumped in and said, "Six creams and six sugars, Mama."

"You got it, baby," she replied. An approving smile would slowly creep across her face. Mama really appreciated that we were willing to go get her a fix for her cravings.

Fifteen years ago it was easy to order a cup of coffee at McDonald's, and over time Mama's coffee preference became second nature to us. Her order was simple because the menu was simple.

If you went into a McDonald's restaurant today, would you find a simple coffee menu? Not a chance. They have twelve coffee options! Heck, I still don't know the difference between a latte and a cappuccino. There are drastic differences between the company's coffee options in 1991 and 2012. Put it this way: I have a set of guidelines I follow whenever my mom asks me to pick up some coffee. She has to text me her *list of ingredients* just to make sure I get the order right. Things certainly have changed.

One of the hallmarks of a fast-track performer is his or her ability to embrace and navigate change. This is a major competency of the twenty-first-century professional. Change is all around you. Change is constant. How well do you deal with workplace change?

A Cautionary Tale of Change Mismanagement

Everyone over the age of twenty-five remembers when Montgomery Ward was a household name in the department-store space. The stores were always busy, and it seemed like it was an institution that would be there forever. Fast-forward twenty years and most ten-year-olds have never heard of Montgomery Ward. How could a pillar of the business community seemingly vanish into thin air?

Montgomery Ward started operations in 1872 as a dry-goods mail-order-catalog business. Midwestern farmers accounted for the majority of its customer base (Wilson et al. 2005), and business was booming. The company enjoyed decades of exponential growth and steady profits. Around 1950, the retail operation began to struggle because it was slow to respond to middle-class families' movement from the city to the suburbs. Sears and Roebuck and J. C. Penney and Company adjusted their business models faster and took market share from Montgomery Ward, marking the beginning of its decline.

Montgomery Ward ran its catalog business until 1985, when it made a stronger push into its retail operation, but Target, Wal-Mart, and K-Mart had moved faster and garnered market share and momentum. Montgomery Ward limped along for another fifteen years until it finally closed in 2000 ("Montgomery Ward Died" 2000). The closure marked the largest retail liquidation in the history of the United States.

This case study is a cautionary tale of what happens when companies fail to incorporate smart and timely change. Montgomery Ward had every reason to change in the 1940s, and again in the 1980s, but it stood pat and played a weak hand too long, letting its competitors gain market share. Change is inevitable and must be embraced. Companies that refuse to adapt might as well write out their epitaphs.

The Good Side of Change

Imagine you have just been promoted to CEO of a fledgling company. You have access to the private jet and generous stock options, and you get to play by your own rules. You are the Man . . . or the Woman. You are on your way to the office for a major strategy meeting. Last year your company lost almost $1 billion, and everyone looks to you for the solution. What's more, your core business has only 2 percent of a very lucrative market. What do you do? You must choose one of three options:

1. Allocate more money to research and development for your core business in an attempt to deliver a high-quality product to a hungry market.
2. Sell the company to a major competitor and part with a nice sum of money.
3. Invest in research and development in new markets outside your core business to create brand excitement and deliver high-quality products to the market.

So which option did you choose? If you chose option A, you went for the safe option. If you chose option B, you decided that one private jet is not enough. That is the American way, right? If you chose option C, your name is Steve Jobs, and you are on your way to leading the most profitable company in the history of the world.

In 1997 Apple recognized it needed a game changer. The company had lost $773 million the previous year, and Steve Jobs thought it was the perfect time to be bold and revolutionize the company's suite of products (Apple 2012). Apple created a team to revolutionize the music player and transform the market, and I can only imagine some of the water-cooler conversations after the company announced this strategic initiative. I am sure people were certain it would fail, thinking there was no way a personal computer company could be successful in the music space. How would you have reacted to this strategy if you had been an Apple employee? Some people probably left the company so that they wouldn't have to worry about the sting of massive layoffs after this crusade came to a tragic end.

You know how this story ends. By the end of 2012, Apple sold 329 million iPods (Statistica 2013). My wife and I have three iPods between the two of us. Of course we both have iPhones too. Steve Jobs knew Apple had to do something different, and his strategy catapulted the technology, music, and cell phone industry into the future.

All Companies Change over Time

Company	Initial Product Suite	Current Product Suite
Apple	Apple I desktop computer	Laptop computers, desktop computers, software, iPhone, iPod, iPad, iTunes, & Apple television
IBM	Commercial scales, industrial time recorders, meat and cheese slicers, tabulators, & punched cards	Personal computers, semiconductors, software, servers, storage, cloud computing, IT services, business consulting, training, & asset recovery
Xerox	Photographic paper	Office equipment, call center management, human resources, communication/marketing, finance/accounting, document management, IT outsourcing, & parking/transportation services
McDonald's	Hamburgers, fries, soda, & milkshakes	Hamburgers, fries, soda, milkshakes, oatmeal, salads, chicken nuggets, chicken wraps, gourmet coffee, smoothies, combo meals, happy meals, dollar menu
Pizza Hut	Pizza & breadsticks	Pizza, wings, calzones, pasta, & dessert
Nike	Running shoes & cleats	All athletic shoes, sports apparel, & sports equipment
AT&T	Local/long distance landline phone service	Local/long distance landline service, cell phone service, digital television, & internet

Figure 6.1

All of the well-known companies in figure 6.1 changed over time. They did not change because their leadership teams were bored but because the health of their businesses required it. Keep in mind that a company's employee base must change before its customer base will ever notice anything is different. That is where you come in.

Perspective from the Top

I find myself becoming more and more flexible in the workplace. Projects, funding, and staff issues never go the way we plan in our heads. Change happens all the time, so I work to embrace it. I find it is very important not to allow my idea of how things are supposed to be get in the way of how things are. Even when I am thrown a curveball, things turn out just fine. I try to stay focused on my goal and work hard. I always say it's the ideas we have in our heads that make us unhappy. I choose to be happy. It also makes sense to focus on the things I can control and ignore what I can't. I find that paying attention to the things I can control gives me a great sense of satisfaction and confidence. It is important to learn the difference between the two: what you can and cannot control.

—M. A-R., executive director, nonprofit, millennial

Of survey respondents, 65 percent say change in the workplace is challenging for them.

Why Do Professionals Fight Change?

People (and companies) fight change like prize fighters defending a title. Change management is a dirty word in some professional circles. We push back against change because change threatens our sense of normalcy.

I am a creature of habit. Every morning I eat a hearty bowl of apples and cinnamon oatmeal with a handful of Craisins. One morning I opened my cabinet and the oatmeal box was empty. Didn't I just buy a box at the grocery store? I panicked! I had a ten o'clock meeting, and I needed a hearty breakfast to help me get through it. I sauntered over to the refrigerator and found a couple of pears and a container of yogurt. Believe it or not, that small change threw me off my game a bit. I wasn't as focused during my meeting even though I wasn't hungry.

Fast-track performers understand that change is part of the business cycle and professional life. Therefore, they anticipate and embrace it. Embracing change provides a high level of differentiation because most professionals are wired to resist change. Too many people focus on what their organizations changed from instead of what they have changed to. Fast-track performers aren't threatened by change because they see it as an opportunity.

Performance, Power, and Prestige

People push back against change because they are concerned that it will reduce their performance, power, and/or prestige. Organizational change adjusts the status quo and ushers in a new set of norms that often require us to change long-held behaviors.

Consider the best performers in your department. What if your organization adopted a change initiative that reduced the importance of their core strengths? For example, a salesman who is good at acquiring a few high-dollar accounts may not like an organizational strategy that emphasizes a high volume of low-dollar accounts. It's a good chance the change will have an adverse impact on the high performer's output. That person may vehemently resist the change to avoid a dip in performance. Who would want to be open to an organizational strategy that is hostile to their individual strengths and performance? You are more likely to find a Green Bay Packers fan cheering for the Chicago Bears than to find a professional who would welcome such a reality.

Most professionals spend their careers searching for more power. That may sound a bit crass, but it is true. Some people characterize their power-grabbing ambitions as a quest for greater responsibility and credibility. No matter the semantics, all roads lead to the desire for more power. What if you headed a department that was slated to be a casualty of an organizational restructuring? Would you be open to the proposed change? Probably not, because the loss of your department means you lose power.

The last threat that comes from change is the loss of prestige. Prestige refers to respect or admiration that comes from a professional's accomplishments, potential, or reputation. There is an erosion of prestige if company resources get reallocated from your division to another one. That action can signal that your accomplishments and potential have diminished. The threat of a loss of prestige causes professionals to defend the status quo and resist the change.

All of these barriers to change stifle the average professional's performance. Fast-track performers recognize the potential adverse impacts of change and adjust to align with the new normal, creating a significant opportunity for differentiation. Change creates rare opportunities for advancement because organizations discover new, unanticipated needs during implementation. Fast-track performers work to become the solution to those newly discovered needs.

> *Develop a laser focus on what your organization is changing to instead of what it is changing from.*

The Sweet Spots of Change Management

Dr. John P. Kotter, a former Harvard Business School professor, founder of Kotter International, and an authority on organizational change management, has written eighteen books on change and leadership. Kotter's eight steps to a successful change initiative (Kotter 2011) is the basis for countless organizational change strategies throughout the world. This eight-step framework, displayed in figure 6.2, presents a great opportunity for fast-track performers to add differentiated value to their organizations.

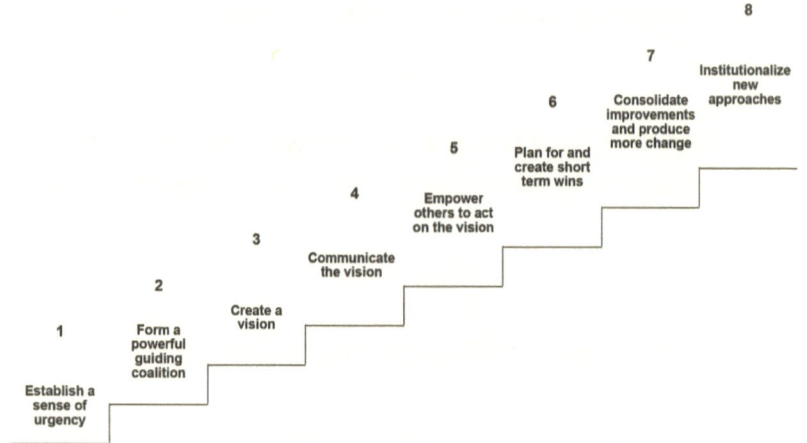

Figure 6.2

Steps 4–7 present the greatest opportunity for fast-track performers to make contributions to their organizations and add differentiated value.

Step 4's Sweet Spot

During step 4 an organization communicates a compelling vision in order to get employee buy-in and alignment for the strategy. Kotter emphasizes the importance of everyone's understanding and acceptance of the change. Fast-track performers ask enough questions to understand why the change is essential and the risks of inaction. If you don't understand the need for the change, you won't be able to fully embrace the change when obstacles arise and the implementation becomes challenging. You can take the following actions to maximize your advantages in this step:

1. Sit down with your boss and other leaders to ask clarifying questions about the change. Make sure you walk away from those conversations with clarity.
2. Share the vision with your coworkers and help get them aligned with the strategy.

Step 5's Sweet Spot

This step is for removing barriers and empowering employees to do their best work in the new structure. Leadership teams often encourage risk-taking and nontraditional activities during change; the rank-and-file employee base is close to the business, so they can think of innovative ways to apply the new strategy new strategy. It is also important that leaders "walk the talk" of the change strategy during this step so that fast-track performers demonstrate their willingness to apply the new strategy to their individual work streams. You can take the following actions to maximize this step:

1. If you are an organizational leader, do the heavy lifting early and immediately begin to live the new strategy.
2. Brainstorm specific actions you must take to reflect the spirit of the change in your daily job responsibilities.

Step 6's Sweet Spot

Step 6, one of the most important in the change-implementation process, focuses on the creation and marketing of quick wins. Everyone has an innate desire to win, but most change initiatives redirect an employee's energy from guaranteed wins to potential wins, which creates uncertainty and resistance.

The Dallas Cowboys became "America's Team" in the 1980s after they won two Super Bowls, thirteen divisional titles, and recorded twenty winning seasons. They gained faithful fans throughout the country because they were winners. People want to align themselves with a winner.

During times of change, organizational leaders mine the company in search of success stories, so the fast-track performer works to become one of those success stories. If you can become a success story, your name will be spread throughout the organization as an example of the possibilities of the new change strategy. Your name will be associated with success and with the future of the company. It is a great opportunity to add considerable value to your organization. You can take the following actions to maximize this step:

1. Become an early adopter of the change initiative.
2. Share your success with your superiors so they can market your efforts.

Step 7's Sweet Spot

Step 7 focuses on adding scale to improvements in order to produce more change. One of the key aspects of this step is to hire, promote, and develop employees who can implement the change vision. This stage is your big payoff if you have been a valuable resource since the inception of the change. Leadership teams want to bring along individuals who understand, support, and perform during change initiatives. Professionals who have aligned with the change have a great opportunity to add more value to their organization in a role with greater responsibility. You can take the following actions to maximize your advantage during this step:

1. Make sure your superiors understand the role you want to play as the change is implemented.
2. Document your track record of success in implementing the change.

Perspective from the Top

I live by the motto that with change comes opportunity. Too many people get stuck in the fear cycle that says change is too scary and they don't want to accept it. I always look to embrace change so I don't get left behind. In 2004 I had been working for about 3.5 years in a profitable division in my company, and things seemed to be going well. Apparently, the company executives did not agree with me, and they decided to shut down my division to cut costs. I was devastated because I had a mortgage and was just laid off from the first job I ever had. I remember that my boss at the time said, "Don't worry about it. You are a smart guy and close to the customer, and you will land on your feet. With change comes opportunity." I now look back on that time eight years later and realize he was right. I ended up in a role with another company, making more money with expanded responsibilities. I was able to increase the trajectory of my career while navigating quite a bit of change.

—S. E., vice president, financial services industry, generation X

Perspective, Perspective, Perspective

Change can be unnerving. It disrupts long-held routines and requires a focused effort to reestablish a sense of normalcy in the workplace. There are so many reasons why we are wired to hate change, but fast-track performers focus on what they can control, not on fighting what they can't control.

All change is not good change, but you won't know that until you give the strategy a try. Not every strategy will work, but every strategy is worth working. Change is going to happen whether you are ready for it or not. Keep organizational change in its proper perspective, and you will empower yourself to quickly buy in and add value to your organization in the process.

The Generational Application

Generation X

Accepting change may be challenging for you. You are closer to the top of the organization and further along in your career than the millennials. You may believe you have a lot to lose during organizational change, but this skill is critical for you. Your ability to navigate and lead through change will lead to many more career advancement opportunities.

You value a portable career and appreciate the ability to move from one company to another with ease. Your career mobility is enhanced by a strong change-management acumen, so change should not be hard for you. You have worked through quite a bit of change: You endured the dot-com crash and multiple recessions. You have a significant amount of experience in strong and weak economies. This is a strength. Take an honest assessment of your perspective of and your comfort level with change in the workplace, and create an action plan to improve any weaknesses.

Millennials

Change should be easy for you. You have lived through the technological revolution, and you change your smartphone every other year (at least) because you don't want to have an outdated device. You typically find change to be exciting because much of your life experience is defined by change.

Your desire for meaning in the workplace is a great source of innovation, and boomers and gen X believe you are incredibly creative and innovative. You have the ability to be a strong catalyst for change, so be proactive and look for ways to change your organization for the better. There are a couple of watch items you should monitor. You may push back against change that doesn't align with your definition of meaningful work, which can cause you to become disengaged and produce low-quality work. One way to mitigate your desire to push back in this way is to seek out the rationale for change. Many organizations struggle to articulate the business imperative for change effectively, so you may just need to ask questions until you understand why the change is important. The answers to your questions may help you create a new way to extract meaning from your work.

These Resources Can Help Right Now

1. *Influencer: The Power to Change Anything* by Kerry Patterson, Joseph Grenny, David Maxfield, and Ron McMillan
2. *Leading Change* by John P. Kotter
3. *Switch: How to Change Things When Change Is Hard* by Chip Heath and Dan Heath
4. *A Sense of Urgency* by John P. Kotter
5. *Our Iceberg Is Melting* by John P. Kotter
6. *Seeing What's Next* by Clayton M. Christensen, Erik A. Roth, and Scott D. Anthony

7. *The Innovator's DNA* by Jeff Dyer, Hal Gregerson, and Clayton M. Christensen

8. *The Innovation Solution* by Praveen Gupta

Be
A
Professional

Advertise
Ambition

Study Your Craft

Be A Change Champion

Build Two-Way Relationships

Communicate Effectively

Perform Consistently

CHAPTER 7

STUDY YOUR CRAFT

"As for me, all I know is that I know nothing."
—Socrates, philosopher

On January 29, 2006, I was in a Charlotte, North Carolina, sports bar screaming and talking major trash to anyone who would listen. I was that obnoxious guy in the bar who wouldn't shut up. The Bears had started Super Bowl XLI with a bang and ran back the opening kickoff for a touchdown. I had every reason to feel good about our start. We needed to strike first because the Indianapolis Colts had Peyton Manning, one of the best quarterbacks ever to play in the National Football League. Of course Manning won his first Super Bowl that night, and the Chicago Bears nation was left with the bitter taste of defeat.

Peyton Manning has developed a reputation as a meticulous strategist and dedicated student of his craft. He knows every offensive play, calls every play on the field for his team, plus he probably knows every defensive play. I wouldn't be surprised if he also knows the tendencies and preferences of *every* defensive player on the field. Many sportswriters have labeled him as the best-prepared athlete of his generation. Manning understands a universal fact of every corporation and organization: people who study their craft are seen as competent experts, as that commitment to your craft translates into performance.

Peyton Manning is not the only one who has figured this out. Think about the salesperson who knows every potential customer objection and can confidently overcome it to sell a product that customers are excited to buy. Simply put, that salesperson took time to be a student of the craft.

Consider the project manager who seems to have a contingency plan for each contingency plan. His or her projects are always completed on time and at or under budget. Those results don't occur by chance; they take hard work and continuous learning. People who take the time to become experts are better equipped to build thriving careers than those who don't, and organizational leaders and HR professionals know it.

Nonperformers take a more passive approach to continuous learning. They wait for their companies to schedule mandatory training, while fast-track performers are always looking for opportunities to learn best practices and new skills. If you want to be a fast-track performer, you have to make a commitment to continuous learning so you can differentiate yourself from your counterparts. The knowledge you gain allows you to add more value to your organization's priorities.

Of survey respondents who remain informed about trends in their industry, 64.6 percent were promoted an average of two times in the last five years.

Knowledge Is Power

This is certainly not the first time you have heard the suggestion to study your craft, but here's a new way to think about how you put this old advice into practice: Break your continuous learning activities into content knowledge and context-knowledge categories. Content knowledge focuses on the technical or functional skills required to execute your responsibilities, while context knowledge targets the variables that impact the environment in which you do your job.

Content Knowledge

Fast-track performers know how to do their jobs well, as they have all the skills required to produce high-quality work. Content knowledge supports your ability to perform and execute your job. For example, project managers may need to understand how to create project work plans, prioritize tasks, and manage their time. Those three skills fall into the content knowledge category because they are requirements for optimal job performance.

Why does content knowledge matter? It allows you to stay ahead of the curve within your area of expertise. Things change all the time as technology continues to streamline and in some cases eliminate traditional processes across industries. As you acquire new skills and strategies, you can share them with your coworkers and become the go-to person for your team in a number of critical functional areas. Do you see value in earning a reputation for always knowing the latest and greatest concept? Reputations like that tend to surface during succession-planning meetings.

Content knowledge development also makes you more marketable in the job market. The new world of career development is all about developing skills with a high degree of portability; the "portfolio" career strategy relies upon a diverse set of functional skills that have broad application to a number of job functions and industries.

The fast-track performer develops the skills for roles that are two or more levels up. Take some time to complete the professional skill audit in figure 7.1. Pay close attention to the final question and be sure to develop a specific action plan with a completion date.

Professional Skill Audit

Key Questions	Answers
What content knowledge does your boss' boss need to have?	
What are some of their critical job responsibilities?	
What are the basic skills required for that role?	
What skills do you already have?	
How can you improve your existing skills?	
What new skills must you acquire?	
How will you develop those new skills?	

Figure 7.1

You can begin to create skill development plans that make you more effective in your current role and more marketable for future roles.

Content Knowledge Development Tips
Conduct a professional skill audit
Pursue a bachelors or advanced degree
Obtain a professional certification or designation
Attend webinars, seminars, or training related to a critical skill development
Look for opportunities to apply new knowledge and skills in the workplace

Figure 7.2

Of survey respondents, 61.3 percent have obtained a certification or professional designation in their field.

Perspective from the Top

I love professional development. Every single staff member on my team has his or her own professional development budget, and we also pool our money together to take classes, lunch-and-learns, and deep investigative visits to learn about a specific issue. For example, we are taking Spanish classes as a group, and we are also going to view a top-tier university for the day in order to understand their admissions process. I view these as valuable tools that will absolutely assist us in achieving our mission. The other option I provide folks is the option to hire a coach. I have personally chosen to do this, and it has been life-changing for me. It is very beneficial to have someone to visit with about my personal and professional challenges. I recognize I don't know everything, so I am always looking for ways to enhance my skills.

—M. A-R., executive director, nonprofit, millennial

Context Knowledge

It is not enough to only know how to perform your job well; you must also know how to do your job well within the context of your department, company, and industry, as well as the overall economy. Fast-track performers understand how their roles fit into their larger organizations.

For example, the day-to-day responsibilities of an accountant at an investment firm may be different from those of an accountant at a trucking company. Of course, the basic skills are transferrable but the context is completely different, so how each accountant adds value to his or her organization may differ. If we are always looking for ways to add differentiated value to our organizations, we must understand what that value looks like. Context knowledge helps us answer that question.

Context knowledge allows you to frame your content knowledge in a way that makes sense for your organization. What role does your business unit play in the larger organizational strategy? Does it generate revenue? Is it a cost or is it a strategic priority? Is it growing or shrinking? These questions help you pinpoint exactly how your business unit connects to the larger organization. Once you know this, you can develop ideas and actions that reinforce your department's organizational position.

After you understand your company's internal strategy, you can begin to focus on the macro variables. It is helpful to know the latest trends and challenges within your industry. For example, if you are in the insurance industry, it may be helpful to know how the industry has responded to the increase in hurricane, tornado, and severe weather activity over the last five years, as that reality has impacted every company in the industry. Fast-track performers have intellectual curiosity about their companies and industries that allows them to strike the right chords with the execution of their daily responsibilities.

One final benefit of context knowledge is that you learn best practices in your industry that you can use to improve your company's performance. This information can spark your creativity and help you develop innovative solutions to organizational challenges. Your ability to benchmark and leverage external resources can be a significant area of differentiation.

Inspiration often comes from unexpected sources. Steve Jobs often roamed department-store appliance aisles looking for fresh design elements for new Apple products. Why would a technology guy immerse himself in appliance design trends? He understood that successful ideas often have broad applications. His intellectual curiosity and relentless focus on continuous learning created a pathway to success. Take some time to think about how you can mine other companies and industries for inspiration.

Context Knowledge Development Tips
Join an industry/professional trade association
Subscribe to magazines within your profession/industry
Listen to company quarterly earnings conference calls (if publicly traded)
Regularly visit company intranet site to learn about important organizational news

Figure 7.3

Of survey respondents, 87.7 percent believe continuous learning is a valuable career-advancement strategy.

Figure 7.4

Companies pay you to have the content knowledge to do your job, but they are more willing to promote you for having the perspective to cut through problems and challenges to find the right path. Content and context knowledge together provide you with a framework to create and execute valuable ideas. Most people don't have the right organizational perspective because they don't have a strategy to seek it out. The combination of context and content knowledge allows you to differentiate yourself from everyone else.

Perspective from the Top

I went from retail to nonprofit to the defense industry. When I applied to my current job, I had no clue about the company or the industry, but in spite of my initial knowledge gap, I have been able to find success in my role. My whole career has been about creating more diverse workplaces to enhance an organization's competitive advantage, and I always looked to connect a more diverse workplace to an organization's mission. Well, that strategy did not work well in my current industry at first. Try getting a bunch of engineers and scientists to care about a warm and fuzzy subject like diversity. I had to learn everything I could about my company and industry. I researched the best practices in the area of diversity within every other company in our industry, and this competitive intelligence shortened my learning curve and allowed me to add value to my company. The best part of continuous learning is the reduction in groupthink. When you have conversations with people outside your company and industry, you always bring a fresh perspective to the table. It also gives you an opportunity to gain access to more influential conversations via happy-hour invitations because you demonstrate a strong understanding of your profession and/or industry. These conversations have been beneficial to me, and I owe it to my relentless focus on learning.

—E. D., senior manager, defense industry, millennial

I Think; Therefore, I Am

You have invested a considerable amount of time in acquiring new knowledge. Now you have to figure out how to capitalize on it. You can use your content and context knowledge to think like a senior leader in your organization, as once you understand the company strategy, you can begin to ask the right questions. What causes your senior leadership team to lose sleep at night? What are the critical issues of the organization? When you understand these issues, you can make sure you don't contribute to the problems and adjust your efforts to be part of the solutions.

You can think like a leader even if you are an individual contributor and don't lead a team of employees. Individual contributors and organizational leaders typically focus on different things: individual contributors think about how they can do their jobs better, while organizational leaders think about how they can do their jobs better *and* get others to do their jobs better. The fast-track performer talks like an organizational leader during meetings and casual conversations with peers, which helps you develop a reputation as someone who "gets it." Your peers and organizational leaders will certainly take notice.

The Generational Application

Generation X

You value constant learning because it helps you maintain a healthy, portable career. You never want your livelihood to be at the mercy of one company. If you maintain a strong skill set, you will always have a competitive résumé to take into the job market, so you can't rest on your laurels. Your newly acquired knowledge will also help you be more effective in your current role. Studying your craft aligns perfectly with your workplace values, although it requires extra effort.

Your work funds your lifestyle, and you definitely don't like your work to dominate your life. However, studying your craft is not so much work as an investment in you and your future happiness and stability.

Millennials

You are an intelligent and competent professional, and you understand that the workplace changes often. You will remain relevant in the workplace as long as your skills remain relevant. Your constant pursuit of knowledge allows you to continue to find new ways to enjoy your work and reinvent yourself, and it provides you with a framework for innovation. Boomers and gen X expect you to innovate, and if you don't look for ways to develop your skills and knowledge, you will fall short of those expectations. You believe the most talented and capable person should get the promotions and high-profile assignments, and if you invest in your skills, you can be the person who gets those opportunities.

These Resources Can Help Right Now

1. Join a professional organization.
2. Pursue a professional certification or designation. Most professional associations have certification programs. These official industry associations verify and validate your skills in a particular area.
3. Subscribe to one or two magazines that serve your industry.
4. Take a class in an area of interest.
5. Go back to school and complete a bachelor's or master's degree program.
6. *What Got You Here Won't Get You There* by Marshall Goldsmith

CHAPTER 8

ADVERTISE YOUR AMBITION

"If I was down to my last dollar, I'd spend it on public relations."
—Bill Gates, business leader

At some point almost everyone has had a conversation about this question: "If a tree falls in the forest and no one is there to hear it, does it make a sound?"

There are two premises that guide my approach to the question.

Premise A

The question is irrelevant and can't be answered because no one has the necessary information to respond intelligently.

Premise B

The question is legitimate and deserves an answer. However, the answer can't be discussed or acted upon because no one has direct knowledge of it.

Here are my responses to the falling-tree question based on premises A and B.

Falling-Tree Response A

If no one is there to hear the tree fall, then whether it makes a sound is irrelevant and insignificant. The question can't be answered because no one was present during the act to discuss the characteristics of the sound.

Falling-Tree Response B

Of course it made a sound because trees always make a noise when they fall. Unfortunately, no one will ever be able to discuss the sound because they are unaware of its occurrence.

There you are. I have finally addressed this question that has given many people a reason to scratch their head. You may be wondering why in the world I am discussing this in a book about career advancement. Let's use the same deconstruction process to analyze an analogous question about your career: "If you want a specific career opportunity and no one knows of your ambition, do you really want it?"

Here are my responses to the career-ambition question based upon premises A and B.

Career-Ambition Response A

If no one knows your ambition, it is irrelevant and insignificant. The question can't be answered because no one has the required knowledge to discuss your desires.

Career-Ambition Response B

Of course you want it because your ambition is a real internal desire. Unfortunately, no one will ever be able to discuss that ambition because they are unaware of its existence.

Fast-track performers have a keen awareness of what they want and make it a point to ensure their leaders thoroughly understand their career goals. The only way anyone will ever know how you envision a thriving career is by your telling them. When you go to a fast-food restaurant, they ask for your order, you tell them, and they prepare it. If you never tell them what you want, you won't get it.

> **Survey respondents listed lack of clarity regarding one's desired career path as one of the most common challenges to career advancement.**

What Do You Really Want?

You must know what you want before you can advertise it. When I was in college, I was often terrified about the future because I did not know what I wanted to do. I knew I wanted to be fulfilled, but I had no clue what fulfillment looked like. I was just as clueless when

I finally stumbled into the workforce, and my first few jobs sucked. Although I did not know what I wanted, I knew those jobs weren't it.

Have you ever been in that situation? It is difficult to plan a career strategy when you don't know where you want to go. You can't rely on your boss to help you because he or she may also lack career clarity, and because no one knows you better than you do.

Let's take some time to think about your interests and priorities. This brainstorming process initiates self-discovery that can be revealing.

Priority-Career Connections

What are the five most important priorities in your life at the moment?

What role does your career play in the achievement of your priorities?

Career-Aspiration Brainstorm

What are you most passionate about? What do you love doing?

Identify the best job you've ever had. What made it so enjoyable?

What do you like most about your current job? The least?

Describe the characteristics of your ideal career.

Review your responses to see if you notice any trends or themes. Do your responses point toward a career category you have yet to consider? Keep in mind that you change and circumstances change all the time, and as your priorities change, your career goals may follow suit. It is a good idea to revisit these questions from time to time to ensure you are moving purposefully toward the career you want.

Of survey respondents, 24.7 percent do not
have a three-to-five-year career plan.

Perspective from the Top

I knew right away that I wanted to move up in the organization, and told this to my leader within several weeks of being hired. I would advise someone who is also looking to advance to be careful of the tone in your conversation and not to expect to move up too quickly. You may have the drive and talent to advance in your organization, but it will not happen overnight. The conversation I had with my boss was to let her know my intent and that I fully expected to have a long learning curve. I needed her to know that I was committed to my career and the organization. I did not expect my opportunity to come instantly. It took a couple of years from that conversation to have that first advancement to management. I wanted her support in learning the competences to get into that role in the future, but I also took it upon myself to develop outside of the workplace. I have done this several times in my career with great success.

—S. H., vice president, higher-education industry, generation X

Words Really Do Matter

Once you have clarity about the direction of your career, it is time to do something with that information. The personnel decision makers in your organization need to know how you want to grow your career. My grandmother always used to say, "A closed mouth doesn't get fed." In other words if I want something, I need to open my mouth and make it known. That was and always will be great advice.

Below you will find two ways to frame your career goals. Review each approach and determine which option is best.

Approach 1: I want to be a member of the management team in order to get more experience leading people in the workplace.

Approach 2: I want to help develop other people's skills to improve their performance, become a reliable resource to leaders during change, and play an integral role in the creation and implementation of organizational strategy.

Do you prefer approach 1 or 2? The first approach is position-specific and treats your career like a destination. This limits your opportunities. Once you get into management, your boss may assume his or her job is done. But your ambition certainly doesn't end with your first management position. As you gain more experience, your ambitions change.

You certainly don't want to get stuck at your first promotion. Fast-track performers take a goal-specific approach to their career planning and identify a series of goals they would like to accomplish during their careers. When you focus on such goals, you make yourself eligible for more opportunities. The best thing about approach 2 is that it has a long shelf life. You may only achieve one of the goals with your next promotion, but your superiors understand that your development has not ended. There are still more goals that need to be accomplished. This approach allows you to plan two or three roles ahead.

Bad-Boss Insurance

Wouldn't it be great if only the best people made it into corporate leadership? Unfortunately, there are many horrible bosses out there who make it tough for their subordinates to go to work every day. Good bosses are easy to work for. They are responsive and fair, recognize good work, maintain accountability, and offer sound feedback to promote employee development. But bad bosses can be pure hell. They take many forms but are essentially the antithesis of a good boss. Bad bosses are a fact of professional life, as everyone will eventually have to endure a bad boss. What do you do if you are working for someone who seems to wake up on the wrong side of the bed every day?

The fast-track performer networks with other leaders to mitigate the adverse effects of a bad boss on his or her career prospects. If left unchecked, a poor relationship with your boss may cause you to get a bad annual performance review. A bad boss can also work to sabotage your career by casting you and your performance in a negative light among their peers and superiors. Organizational leaders tend to give a lot of weight to the perspective of an employee's boss since a manager has many interactions with his or her employees and can speak firsthand about performance issues.

If you network with other leaders, and your boss speaks ill of you in a succession-planning meeting, the other leaders in your network may speak up to share their perspective of your work.

Of survey respondents, 53.8 percent have discussed career ambitions with organizational leaders other than their boss.

Your Board of Directors

Every company has a board of directors that serves as advisors to help the company stay on track and live its mission and vision statements. Although are not a Fortune 500 company, your career is so important that you should also createyour very own board of directors. An ideal board is a cadre of sponsors within your organization who know you, are willing to act on your behalf, and give you advice. They typically hold higher positions in your organization and often sit at the decision-making table.

The privilege to assemble a board of directors is earned, but fast-track performers can recruit boards that are willing to act on their behalf because board members want to align themselves only with high performers. They are too busy to put a hamster-wheel performer on their radar. You have to stand out. You have to add differentiated value.

Inform your board of directors of your career goals and solicit their feedback. If they know what you want to accomplish in your next few roles, they will be able to serve as internal career advisors and recommend you for opportunities that align with your ambition. Your board doesn't guarantee you a promotion, but it does increase the likelihood that you will have representation during personnel discussions.

These are high-quality relationships. Don't overuse them. You should only bring major questions or concerns to them because they are too busy to answer twenty questions per day. Use them sparingly.

The board can be particularly useful during times of organizational change because you can reach out to them if you need clarity on the change initiative to shorten your learning curve.

Your board of directors should be a diverse set of well-respected people across departments and levels of leadership. It is important to diversify your board by department because you don't know where your career path may take you. Cast a wide net to maximize the functionality of your board.

Identify Your Resources

Complete the grid in figure 8.1 by listing the names of the people resources in your company that correspond to each box. The categories on the left side represent situations or events, while the categories on the top represent the area in which the situation occurs. For example, the top-left box contains the names of people you reach out to when you need clarity about professional or career-related issues, while the bottom right contains the people you reach out to when you want to celebrate achievements in the area of organizational strategy.

	Professional & Career	Organizational Strategy
Need Clarity		
During Crisis		
Celebrate Achievements		

Figure 8.1

Do you remember the Relationship Check-Up exercise you completed in chapter 5, in which you listed all of the people with whom you need to have viable two-way relationships? Do you have some of the same people listed in the grid in figure 8.1? Ideally, you would like these two lists to overlap somewhat. If you don't have much overlap, take time to evaluate what you may need to change in order to build more consistent relationships.

The Generational Application

Generation X

Advertising your ambitions is an opportunity to share your career expectations with your superiors. Even if you are not sure how long you will remain with your current employer, you want to maximize your opportunity while you are there. You must be aware of what you want to accomplish during your tenure at a specific job or company. Do you need to take a lateral move to broaden your résumé for your next opportunity? What type of opportunity would lead you to leave your current company? It is important for you to understand your career strategy so you can remain opportunistic. Once you know what you want to do and how long you want to do it, use your communication skills to relay that message to your superiors.

Millennials

Your biggest challenge is to figure out what you want. You may be interested in a number of things, but take the time to understand what you value in your career. Once you figure this out, you can begin to develop your strategy to communicate your desires to your superiors.

You face a few perception headwinds that you must reconcile. First, boomers and gen X believe you have an unhealthy sense of entitlement, perhaps because you were raised during some of the best economic years of the last century when your parents got jobs with ease and maximized their purchasing power. Well, that was then and this is now. The Great Recession changed things, and we are in an economic period that requires patience.

There is also a perception among boomers and gen X that you have unrealistic expectations of career advancement. Boomers and gen X understand it takes time to build a thriving career, that you have to invest in your career and pay your dues to some degree. Be cognizant of these perceptions as you share your career ambition with your superiors. Be honest about your goals, but make sure they understand you have the right perspective.

These Resources Can Help Right Now

1. *Manage Your Manager: How to Get Ahead with Any Type of Boss* by Gonzague Dufour
2. *It's Okay to Manage Your Boss* by Bruce Tulgan
3. *How to Ask for a Raise without Getting Fired* by Lawrence D. Schwimmer
4. *Get Paid! Secrets to Negotiating Your Salary and Getting Paid What You're Worth* by Stacy Michelle

CHAPTER 9

BE A PROFESSIONAL

"Professionalism is like love; it is made up of the constant flow of little bits of proof that testify to devotion and care."
—Thomislav Sola, author

You have implemented all of the major strategies of the fast-track performer. Now it is time to add the final layer of your career-advancement strategy. An aura of professionalism is just as important as consistent performance, as your professionalism speaks to how you go about executing your job responsibilities.

Look the Part

Let's say you are on the management team at Acme Windows and Glass, and you are set to interview two people for an open account manager position that reports to you. Look at each picture below and write down your perceptions of the candidates' work quality, background, and ability to execute the account manager responsibilities.

List your thoughts about image A below.

List your thoughts about image B below.

You probably had a more favorable reaction to image B than to image A. What is the source of the positive reaction? Based on their attire, the group looks like competent professionals. Is it fair to draw such strong conclusions because someone has good fashion sense? Perhaps not, but we must deal with the world as it is.

Physical appearance matters. What does your attire say about you? How do you dress when you go into the office every day? Do you look like a professional or an amateur? The boomers coined the phrase, "Dress for the job you want, not the job you have." That phrase still has currency in the new workforce.

The One-Plus Rule

Dress codes become more casual every day. Certainly, the suit-and-tie workplace is far less common today than it was twenty-five years ago. You stand out in a sea of khaki pants and polo shirts if you implement "the one-plus rule." Simply put, you consider your company dress code as the baseline and adopt the dress code that is one level higher than that baseline. For example, if your company dress code is casual, you adopt a business-casual standard. This mode of dress is still close enough to the standard that you won't be conspicuously overdressed but enough above it that you have a strong point of visual differentiation. It may not be as important as it once was to wear three-piece suits or pantyhose, but a professional's attire still matters.

Are there people in your office with whom you have never worked, perhaps because they are in another department, but you've developed a perception of them? What is the basis of your perception? Does their attire have any part in forming that perception? I'll bet it does—and guess what? They also have a perception of you. They may know someone who works closely with you, or they may have seen a report you produced, but there is also a good chance that your attire is the source of at least part of their perception.

We have talked throughout this book about the importance of perceptions in the workplace and how you must manage your perceptions or those perceptions will manage you.

Watch the Clock

My brother Michael is a member of the Marine Corps. When he went to basic training some years ago, he was a nervous kid who did not know what was in store for him. What lessons would he learn? Would he meet new friends? I always heard horror stories about boot camp, so of course I was concerned. Little brothers are supposed to worry, right? Well, one of the first lessons Michael learned was to hurry up and wait. The idea is to be early so you have to wait to be on time.

This lesson applies nicely to your career. Have you ever joined a meeting two to three minutes late and everyone stares at you when you enter the room? How bad does that feel? Let's face it. No one wants to be that guy! Can you think of a colleague who is always late? If you can think of him or her, I am sure other coworkers can as well. That person has a high level of differentiation but for the wrong reason.

What does tardiness say about the quality of a person's work or about how he or she values others' time? Baby boomers and gen X both value timeliness. If your boss or other superiors are members of those two generations, you may want to adopt the hurry-up-and-wait approach to timeliness. Be on time for work, face-to-face meetings, and conference calls. Promptness is the mark of a professional. Although the workforce is in a state of significant change, the importance of this behavior will not change. Timeliness does not require a sophisticated skill set; it just requires your commitment.

Of all survey respondents 63 percent said
they almost never arrive late to work.

Beat the Deadline

Deadlines are important and must always be met, but too many employees and leaders treat deadlines as though they were optional. The fast-track performer understands that deadlines are important and must always be respected.

Do you understand the rationale for the deadline your boss gave you last week? I look at deadlines as the fuel that powers the operational engine of an organization, as deadlines force progress. Without them, a project can become stagnant and lose momentum. Deadline discipline is critically important to the construction of a thriving career.

If deadlines are so important, why do most people only seek to meet them? Imagine you are the project manager of a high-profile initiative in your organization. Since one of the primary concerns of a project manager is completing the project on time, you assigned project deliverables to your team of ten employees with clear deadlines. Two members of your team completed their work two days early, seven completed their work on time, and one missed the deadline.

What is your reaction to each group? The early group exceeded your expectations and helped make your job easier. They fall into the fast-track-performer category because they beat the deadline, which differentiates them from everyone else.

The on-time group did exactly what you asked them to do. You appreciate their efforts, but are you as impressed with them as you are with the early group? Assuming the quality of everyone's work is equal, they did not give you a reason to be impressed as it relates to the deadline. This group does not stand out, so it falls into the run-of-the-mill-performer category.

The late group is memorable for the wrong reason. You will remember them because they made your job more difficult, and you will probably not be excited about working with them on a future project. People who miss deadlines create more work for their colleagues and cause unnecessary stress. Do you think employees with that label have a difficult time building a thriving career? This group falls into the nonperformer category.

What would it take for you to beat most of your deadlines? You probably need to focus on your time-management and task-prioritization skills and find a reliable system that allows you to beat your deadlines consistently. Get to work and make this behavior part of your career-development strategy. Let me leave you with one word of caution: Do not sacrifice quality for speed.

The Generational Application

Generation X

You value a laid-back work environment that is free from unnecessary structure, but you appreciate the opportunity to work with professionals. If you appreciate working with professionals, you should be professional as well. Your time is important to you, so be on time to indicate you respect others' time as well. This strategy should be easy for you, as it reflects your values.

Millennials

Company dress codes changed when you joined the workforce. Gen X started the trend, but you have taken it to the next level. As a result, you have a significant opportunity to differentiate yourself from your peers who do not know how to dress professionally.

You should not have any challenges with timeliness. If you enjoy the work you do, will be prompt and timely in your communications and actions. This is a quick win for you.

These Resources Can Help Right Now

1. Get to work and meetings early, and use the extra time to get to know your colleagues and build meaningful relationships. Remember: those two-way relationships matter.
2. *Five Steps to Professional Presence* by Susan Bixler and Lisa Scherrer Dugan
3. *Executive Presence: The Art of Commanding Respect Like a CEO* by Harrison Monarth
4. *Seeing Yourself as Others Do: Authentic Executive Presence at Any Stage of Your Career* by Thomas Mungaven
5. *Creating Personal Presence: Look, Talk, Think, and Act Like a Leader* by Dianna Booher

CHAPTER 10

PUTTING IT ALL TOGETHER

"A journey of a thousand miles begins with a single step."
—Lao Tzu, philosopher

You have spent a considerable time now thinking about the ideal behaviors that lead to a thriving career. You have completed activities and exercises and read relevant stories and anecdotes. This guide provides many tips and tactics that can add value to your career-development strategy. However, some people will get to the last chapter of this book and never make progress toward implementing its strategies. Will you fall into that category, or will you work to put the strategies into practice?

You've turned page after page and finally made it to the last chapter. Now is the time to think about application and execution. I invite you to put it all together and make a significant down payment on your thriving career.

Define Your Brand

Remember that you are the CEO of You, Inc. You are not only an employee. You are more than just a professional. You are your own brand, and your employer is your primary customer. To clarify this concept of you as a brand, let's first define a brand.

According to *Advertising, Promotion, and Other Aspects of Integrated Marketing* (Shimp 2010), a brand is everything that a product or service stands for in comparison to other brands in similar categories; it represents a consistent set of values. Your behavior and performance should make a strong, clear, and consistent statement about you. That statement is your brand.

It is not enough just to have a defined brand in the workplace. You must also develop a sufficient amount of brand equity, which refers to the extent to which people are familiar with your brand and associate favorable, strong, and unique thoughts with it.

Take a few moments to write down the thoughts and feelings that immediately come to mind when you think of one of your parents.

_____   _____

_____   _____

_____   _____

Everything that came to mind can be categorized as this parent's brand equity. Now write down what you think your coworkers would write if I asked them for the thoughts and feelings that immediately come to mind when they think of you. What adjectives do you think they will use to describe your value? What adjectives would you like them to mention?

_____   _____

_____   _____

_____   _____

Be intentional about building your brand and your brand equity. First, determine what words you want people to associate with your brand. Second, identify the actions you must take to create your desired brand associations. Third, identify the actions you must avoid in order to create your desired brand associations.

Your brand matters. The decision makers in your organization, whether they realize it or not, think about your brand when they evaluate your readiness for the next promotion. You are in complete control of how you are perceived. Think through how the seven competencies outlined in the Promotion Pyramid can help you create and reinforce your brand.

Create Your Action Plan

The well-known euphamism "Knowledge is power" is incomplete. A more appropriate statement is "Knowledge properly applied is power." Two things must happen in order for you to maximize the content of this guide. First, you must make a commitment to apply the concepts that resonate with you and begin to build the thriving career that you want and deserve. Progress is impossible if you fail to take action.

After you take action, you must be sure to evaluate the effectiveness of your action. Not all action is created equal. When I was a sophomore at Bradley University, I played golf a few times with some of my buddies. My drive off the tee was a perfect straight line. Sounds like a promising sign, right? That was the silver lining to a pretty ugly rain cloud because the distance on my drive was only sixty yards! Something about my golf game was ineffective, and if I wanted to improve, I'd need a swing coach.

The point of the story is this: I had to first acknowledge my ineffectiveness before I could improve my results. The same principle applies to your career-development action plan. Evaluate your effectiveness and correct your course as necessary. You can use the grid in figure 10.1 to create your action plan.

Your Action Plan Template

Targeted Competency	Specific Actions for Improvement	Deadline for Completion	Actual Date of Completion
Consistently Perform			
Communicate Effectively			
Build Two-Way Relationships			
Be a Change Champion			
Study Your Craft			
Advertise Your Ambition			
Be a Professional			

Figure 10.1

THE FUTURE BELONGS TO YOU

The workforce is in the midst of a major transformation, and too many gen X and millennial professionals find themselves unprepared to capitalize on the organic movement that has already begun. You are at a major career crossroads. You can join the ranks of the fast-track performers by implementing a strategy that leads to a thriving career, or you can adopt the more common trial-and-error approach that leads to frustration and missed opportunities.

The future is yours if you implement the right strategy. This guide is the blueprint that will help you build the thriving career you want, need, and deserve. I wish you the absolute best as you embark upon this critical journey.

BIBLIOGRAPHY

Apple. 2012. "Company History 1996–1997." http://apple-history. com/h6.

Burg, Bob, and John David Mann. 2007. *The Go-Giver: A Little Story about a Powerful Business Idea*. New York: The Penguin Group.

Carnegie, Dale. 1936. *How to Win Friends and Influence People*. New York: Simon and Schuster.

Coon, Larry. "Lockout: What Will the Players Do Next?" 2011. http://espn.go.com/nba/story/_/page/nextforplayers-111114/ nba-players-do-next.

Gibson, Christina, and Kirkman Bradley. 2012. "Our Past, Present, and Future in Teams: The Role of Human Resource Professionals in Managing Team Performance across Cultures." http://ceo. usc.edu/pdf/G9813341.pdf.

Gladwell, Malcolm. 2002. *The Tipping Point: How Little Things Can Make a Big Difference*. New York: First Back Bay.

Harrison, Ratiera. 2008. "Closing the Knowledge Gap: Retention of the Transitory Employee." *Journal of Contract Management* (Summer): 49–59. http://www.ncmahq.org/files/Articles/JCM08 —pages 49-59.pdf.

Kotter, John P. 2011. *Leading Change: Why Transformation Efforts Fail. Harvard Business Review's Ten Must Reads on Change*. Boston: Harvard Business School.

Lancaster, Lynne, and David Stillman. 2002. *When Generations Collide: Who They Are. Why They Clash. How to Solve the Generational Puzzle at Work.* New York: HarperCollins.

_____. 2010. *The M-Factor: How the Millennial Generation Is Rocking the Workplace.* New York: HarperCollins.

Medina, John. 2008. *Brain Rules: Twelve Principles for Surviving and Thriving at Work, Home, and School.* Seattle: Pear Press.

"Montgomery Ward Died because of Modern Market." 2000. *Seattle Post-Intelligencer,* December 30.

"Neuroscience Institute Studies Neuron Synchronization and Brain Focus." 2005. *Science Letter* (May 24): 1241. http://search. proquest.com/docview/ 209233386?accountid=35812.

Pauker, Lance. 2011. "NBA Power Rankings: The Fifty Most Clutch Players of All Time." *The Bleacher Report* (January 4). http:// bleacherreport.com/articles/ 559446-nba-power-rankings-the-50-most-clutch-players-of-all-time.

Shimp, T. A. 2010. *Advertising, Promotion, and Other Aspects of Integrated Marketing Communications* (8th ed.). Mason, OH: South-Western Cengage Learning.

Smith, Michael. 2006. "McNabb: T. O. Situation Was about Money, Power." http://sports.espn.go.com/nfl/news/story?id=2315565.

Society for Human Resource Management. 2009. "2009 Employee Job Satisfaction Survey Report." http://www.shrm.org/ Research/SurveyFindings/Articles/Documents/09-0282_Emp_ Job_Sat_Survey_FINAL.pdf.

Statista. 2013. "Global Apple iPod Sales Q1 2006–Q1 2013." http:// www.statista.com/statistics/12769/worldwide-apple-ipod -sales-since-1st-quarter-2006/.

_____. 2012. "Gross Revenue of New York Broadway Shows 2006– 2012." http://www.statista.com/statistics/193006/broadway -shows-gross-revenue-since-2006/.

The Numbers. 2011. "Movie Market Summary for Year 2011." http://www.thenumbers.com/market/2011/summary.

US Bureau of Labor Statistics. 2013. "Employment Status of the Civilian Noninstitutional Population by Age, Sex, and Race." http://www.bls.gov/cps/cpsaat03.htm.

_____. 2012. "Civilian Labor Force by Age, Sex, Race, and Ethnicity." http://www.bls.gov/news.release/ecopro.t01.htm.

Valentine, Craig, Mitch Meyerson, and Patricia Fripp. 2009. *World Class Speaking: The Ultimate Guide to Presenting, Marketing and Profiting like a Champion*. Garden City, NJ: Morgan James Publishing.

Wilson, Mark, Stephen Porter, and Janice Reiff. 2005. "Ward (Montgomery) & Co." http://www.encyclopedia.chicagohistory.org/pages/2895.html.